NETWORK KNOW-HOW: CONCEPTS, CARDS & CABLES

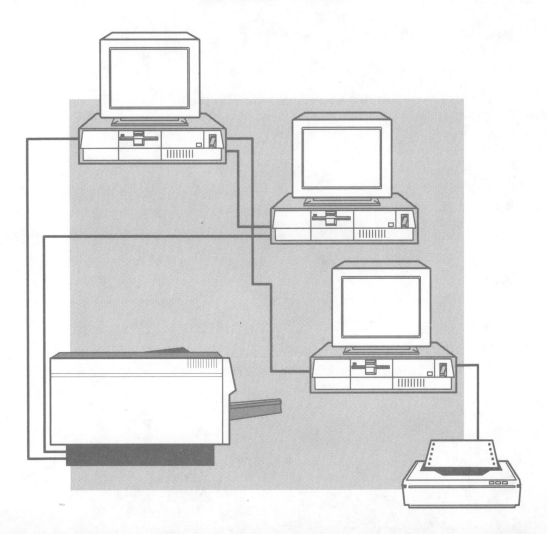

NETWORK KNOW-HOW: CONCEPTS, CARDS & CABLES

Dan Derrick

Osborne **McGraw-Hill**

Berkeley New York St. Louis San Francisco
Auckland Bogotá Hamburg London Madrid
Mexico City Milan Montreal New Delhi Panama City
Paris São Paulo Singapore Sydney
Tokyo Toronto

Osborne **McGraw-Hill**
2600 Tenth Street
Berkeley, California 94710
U.S.A.

For information on translations or book distributors outside of the
U.S.A., please write to Osborne **McGraw-Hill** at the above address.

Network Know-How: Concepts, Cards & Cables

1234567890 DOC 998765432

ISBN 0-07-881833-8

Publisher
Kenna S. Wood

Acquisitions Editor
William Pollock

Associate Editor
Vicki Van Ausdall

Technical Editor
Ivan Luk

Project Editor
Erica Spaberg

Copy Editor
Dusty Bernard

Proofreader
Janet Walden

Computer Designer
Helena Charm

Illustrator
Susie C. Kim

Cover Designer
Mason Fong

Dedicated to my parents, Jim and Bette Derrick, who still remind me about failing Composition 101 (twice).

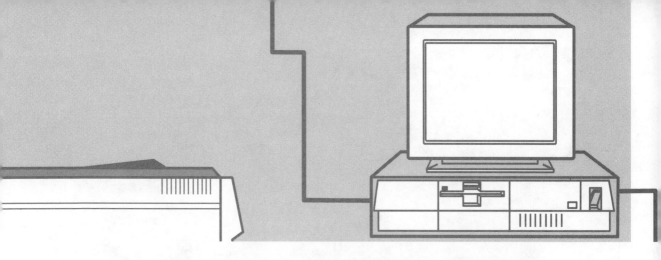

CONTENTS AT A GLANCE

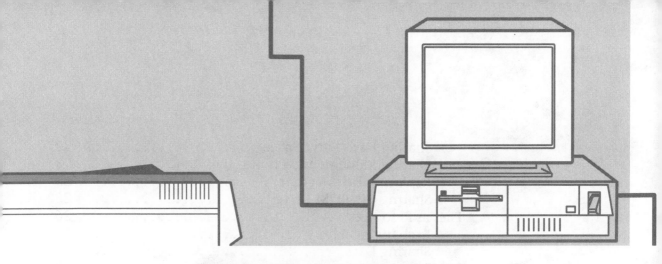

CONTENTS

ACKNOWLEDGMENTS

Writing is only the first of many steps necessary to publishing a book. Standing behind the author is a team of experts who take these rough ideas and make them more readable for everyone. Special thanks to:

✦ Bill Pollock (who hates to talk on answering machines but leaves long speeches anyway);

✦ Ivan Luk (who went beyond being a technical editor to provide many great suggestions);

✦ Vicki Van Ausdall (who likes to call several times a day to see if I'm really writing);

✦ Deborah Craig (who must own stock in a post-it company);

✦ Dusty Bernard (who had a very delicate way with my words);

✦ Erica Spaberg (who has her own way of keeping things on schedule); and

✦ Everyone at Osborne/McGraw-Hill for all their hard work to get this book on the shelves and into your hands.

Thanks to my friends for their advice and encouragement: Marilyn Carmony, Leo Doyle, Andy Pickett, Jo Spangler, and my brother, Dennis Derrick. They all provided ideas and network experiences, many of which are included in this book.

And, as always, a special thanks goes to my wife, Cathy, and our children, T.J. and Rachael. The children are finally old enough that they have stopped asking: When is Daddy going to get a real job?

INTRODUCTION

Written for the potential small network administrator (among others), *Network Know-How: Concepts, Cards & Cables* explains the advantages and disadvantages of a two- to ten-station local area network (LAN). This book provides basic network concepts and tips for installing, testing, and maintaining a small network. These pages provide an overview of the process and help you determine if you can actually install the network yourself.

If you decide to have someone else install the network, you'll be particularly interested in the last chapter. With your newfound understanding of networks and the information in this chapter, you'll save both time and money when dealing with a network consultant.

While most network programs provide instructions for installing the software, those instructions assume you have already plugged in the cards and run the cable and that you know exactly how your network will be set up. This book provides information about all the steps necessary for getting a network up and running, starting with the most important step: planning the network.

NOTE: While several network products are mentioned in this book, they are used to provide specific examples and may not be the best products for your needs.

How this Book Is Organized

Some computer books are written as a reference, consulted only when a problem occurs. Others provide step-by-step instructions for completing specific tasks. Some, like this one, provide general concepts that you can apply to your own experiences.

Take a few lunch hours or a quiet afternoon and read this book from front to back. If you protest that you don't have the time to read this book from cover to cover, then you certainly don't have time to install, test, and maintain a network. Think of the reading time as a compound investment. That time will be paid back again and again by the problems you will avoid as you install and use your network.

Whether or not you will be installing the network yourself, make this book an interactive document. Write notes in the margins. Put post-its on pages you want others to notice. Pass this book along (with your notes) to everyone involved in the network process. (Of course, you can buy everyone a copy to read to save time.) This book can be the common seed for starting your network's growth.

The chapters include worksheets and checklists to help you determine if you need a network, how to plan for one, and how to install one. Here is an overview of each chapter:

✦ Chapter 1, "Considering a Small Network," defines networks from an administrator and user perspective. It includes a checklist for determining your need for a network.

✦ Chapter 2, "Advantages and Disadvantages of Networked Computers," describes how a network can help people work together. The chapter also discusses how a network can complicate computer use. A checklist helps you determine if you are ready for a network.

✦ Chapter 3, "Can You Install a Network?," prepares you for the process of installing a network. This chapter includes steps for gathering your resources in the process. A checklist helps you determine if you can install the network or if you need to hire a consultant.

✦ Chapter 4, "Network Components," focuses on the basic building blocks in a network. The worksheet in this chapter helps you determine what components you have to work with.

✦ Chapter 5, "Planning the Network," develops a plan for installing the network. An extensive checklist helps you prepare for the first draft of your network plan.

✦ Chapter 6, "Installing Network Hardware," describes the physical installation of the network, including tips on throwing cable and creating connections. There is a checklist for proper card and cable connections.

✦ Chapter 7, "Software Installation," describes network software installation and suggests a "testing" approach. User training is discussed and an outline for a three-hour user orientation session is provided. There is a checklist for both pre- and post-installation activities.

✦ Chapter 8, "Network Maintenance," lists tasks for keeping the network running smoothly, including backing up data and keeping users informed. The checklist helps you determine network maintenance schedules.

✦ Chapter 9, "Working with a Consultant," presents a step-by-step process for finding and dealing with a consultant. The chapter includes an extensive worksheet to help you deal with all aspects of hiring and working with a consultant.

This book is based on the many small networks I've installed and supported over the years. I've taken my hundreds of hours of experience and my conversations with dozens of network administrators and consultants and compressed them into a few hours of reading. I hope my investment pays off for you. Please feel free to contact me through Osborne/McGraw-Hill with any comments or suggestions you have about this book.

CHAPTER

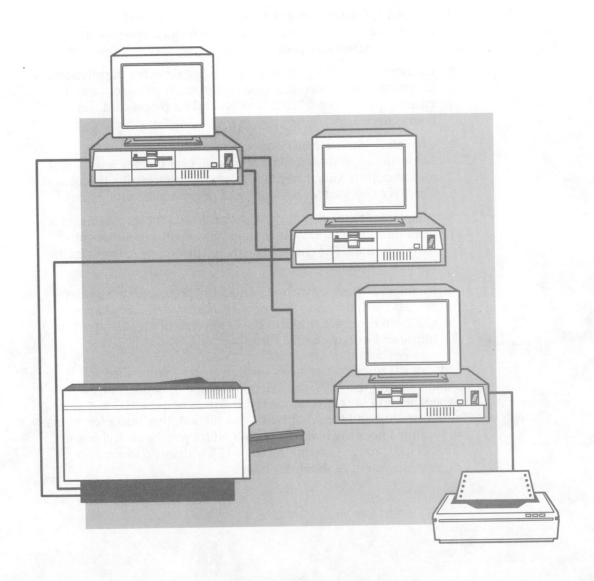

1

CONSIDERING A SMALL NETWORK

Personal computers are becoming easier to connect together. Once connected, they form a network. This chapter explains basic networking concepts. Types of networks are covered with a focus on the smaller networks containing ten or less computer systems. Both the administrator and user perspectives are explored. A checklist at the end of the chapter helps determine if you can justify installing a small network.

A *network* consists of two or more computers connected to exchange data or share resources. This chapter provides an overview of networks, including descriptions of several types of networks. The end of the chapter contains a checklist to determine whether a network would be valuable to your organization.

Defining Networks

When a computer is connected to another computer, both computers are part of a network. The connection can be a phone line or network cable. The computer on the other end may be in the next room or halfway around the world. The connection provides additional file-storage space, another printer, or other resources. The connecting computer is more useful because it also has the enhanced capabilities provided by the main computer.

The original computer shares parts of itself as *resources*. These resources include hard disk space, program and data files, printers, and other devices. All these resources must be designated as part of the network. The more powerful the computer, the more resources it can share with other computers.

Of the many types of networks, one is a *local area network,* abbreviated *LAN.* This network uses personal computers on both ends of the connection. One system may be dedicated to providing the resources, or each computer system may share resources with each other system. Depending on the software, a LAN can contain from two to over a thousand computers. The small networks discussed in this book range from two to ten connected computers.

When personal computers are connected to a LAN, the terms used to describe the systems change. When a computer is used only to provide the resources shared on a network, it is called a *server.* The server, also referred to as the *host,* manages the network and may be a computer just like the others on the network. If the other systems use the server a lot, that computer needs to be more powerful to keep the network running quickly. Some companies provide computers designed to work as servers. These systems can cost over $10,000 and are not necessary for a small LAN.

The term used to define these small computers has changed as the result of networks. Originally the term "personal computer" reflected the fact that only one person could use the system at one time. With the advent of networks, that is no longer true. The more common term for these systems now is *desktop computer*.

When the desktop computer is connected to a network, it becomes a *workstation*. This term indicates that additional resources are now available to that desktop computer. Other terms, such as *node* and *client*, are also frequently used to describe a workstation.

Figure 1-1 contains a diagram of a network, with each part of the network labeled. Notice that both the workstation and server are desktop computers. The difference occurs in their functions on the network. In this example, the server shares resources, while the workstations just use those resources. Other network systems, as explained later in this chapter, allow each workstation to also share resources across the network.

The most common term for a person using a computer, networked or not, is *user*. The user's skills may range from data entry to managing the

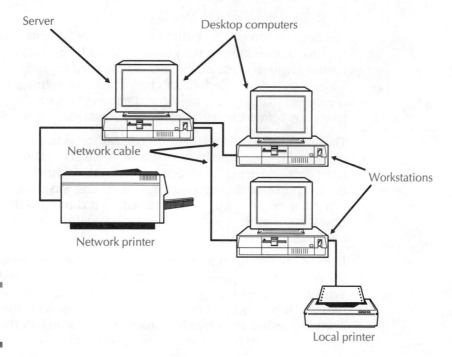

A basic
network
Figure 1-1.

network. In a network, a user has access to the network from a workstation. The level of access is determined by the person who manages the network.

The *supervisor,* also called the *network administrator* or *network manager,* is responsible for the network, and usually is the person who designed and supervised the installation. The supervisor has access to all parts of the network and controls the settings and restrictions for each user on the network.

The limits set for each user define the user's *access level.* Most networks are designed so that the supervisor can restrict the resources available to a user. This prevents users from accidentally accessing or deleting other users' files. The access level can also specify which printers will be used.

A network, then, consists of one or more servers providing workstation access to shared resources. Individual users have varying levels of access to these network resources, based on the network design and management by the supervisor.

The Evolution of Networks

The original computers, built in the 1940s, filled large rooms and required a team of specialists to maintain. All data was kept in these central computers (called *mainframes*), located far away from the users. To get a new report, individuals had to ask the technicians who ran the computers to design the report. If the project list was long, it might take years before the report could be generated.

The advent of terminals made individual access to the mainframe possible. *Terminals* use keyboards and monitors to allow individuals to enter data and generate reports. All terminals connected to, and relied on, the host (server) computer. All processing was done on the main computer, while the users just "talked" to it through a terminal. The host was the critical part of the system, and if the host quit running, no one could do any computing.

In the early 1980s, computer users declared their independence from the corporate computer world when they bought personal computers. With these computers, purchased for less than the cost of a long business trip, people could do what they wanted with the data. The ability to gather and organize information was now in the hands of individuals. Computing had become "personal."

1

For the first few years, desktop computer users were content to keep their data to themselves. If they wanted to share their data, they passed around a floppy disk containing the data files, which only worked if the recipient used the same type of computer and the same program to work with the data. This changed in the mid-'80s, when it became possible to network desktop computers. Companies such as NOVELL developed software and hardware combinations to allow PCs to exchange data. However, not unlike the first desktop computers, the networks were difficult to install and troubleshoot.

The LAN momentum built as installation became easier. Costs came down and more application software became networkable. As networks became popular, users began to depend on shared resources and data, and the networks grew to include more users and more applications. With the trend of *downsizing,* or moving the company's mainframe programs and data onto a LAN-based system and shutting the mainframe down, networks have continued to grow in size. This process typically involves dozens if not hundreds of workstations and includes many servers spread across departments, buildings, and possibly the world. When networks like these are built, network specialists are required to construct a system to support everyone within the company.

Building a network with hundreds of workstations and several servers across the state is not your mission. You just want to connect together a few desktop computers, share the laser printer, and exchange a few E-mail messages. You just want to extend everyone's computing power by making a few network connections.

Types of Networks

Networks can connect two computers on the same desk or connect computers around the world. The type of connection designates the type of network, two of which are LANs and WANs.

LANs

Connecting systems in one office or building creates a local area network (LAN). The server is close, and the workstations make the connection directly to that server.

A larger LAN may have more than one server. These servers have special connections, called *bridges* and *routers,* between them to allow resources to be shared across servers. For example, if you want to use a file located on Server B but your system is physically connected to Server A, you can still reach that data by making the request through Server A, which then sends the request to Server B. The data returns by the same route. Clearly, adding a second server to your LAN significantly increases its complexity. This type of multiserver network is referred to as a *multiserver LAN.*

For example, a larger LAN might have a server located in the accounting department with 15 workstations. The accounting software and data are located on that system. The shipping department may also have a LAN with 8 workstations connected to it. This server runs the inventory and shipping-schedule software. All data to be passed between the workstations in both departments uses a bridge between the servers. When someone in accounting wants to send E-mail to someone in shipping, the transmission goes first to the accounting server, then to the shipping server, and finally to the E-mail recipient in shipping. Figure 1-2 illustrates this multiserver LAN.

WANs

When the data signals extend beyond a LAN, the system has grown to a *wide area network (WAN).* These network connections may include high-speed phone lines, microwaves, or satellites. Needless to say, WANs require a multidisciplinary team of experts to install and manage.

The multiserver LAN example with the accounting and shipping departments would be considered a WAN if the departments were in

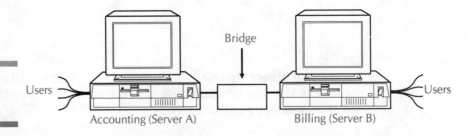

A LAN with
two servers
Figure 1-2.

different cities (or in different buildings). The link between the two servers could be a leased phone line or other transmission method. Depending on the transmission speed, the data exchange between the two servers could take a few minutes or be hardly noticeable. Figure 1-3 shows a sample WAN.

These perspectives provide some idea of the growth possible with a LAN. In fact, you may find that you set up a LAN in your department, stabilize it, and then receive a request to bridge to another department with a LAN. If your company has planned this growth and made sure the networks are compatible, this may be a relatively easy task for someone with experience in this area. If the suggestion is made after both LANs have been established, be prepared for the worst. As with any network strategy, make sure you don't become dependent on the other department's system to keep yours running.

Basic Network Concepts

By definition, desktop computers sit on a desk and do not rely on any other connection (except power) to operate. They are self-contained. You can establish connections between a desktop computer and other systems by using expansion cards in the computer or even just the serial/parallel ports. The variables in the network include the server/workstation software, the type of cable used, and the way that cable is connected to the computer. While each of these factors is covered in later chapters, an overview of the process provides a framework for your network.

At its most basic, two or more computers are connected with a wire. One of the computers (the server) monitors the signals on the wire.

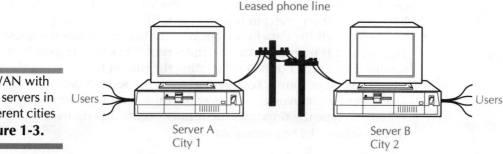

A WAN with two servers in different cities
Figure 1-3.

Leased phone line

Users

Users

Server A
City 1

Server B
City 2

When other computers (workstations) want to use something on the server, they make a request to the server. Depending on the current activities, the server will respond either sooner or later.

At the user level, the only evidence of this transaction may be the slight (or long) delay in making the request. If the request is to load a program from the server and the server is very busy, it takes longer for the program to load. Once the program is loaded at the workstation, the program runs just like it would on a stand-alone computer. The only delay when dealing with a network is when data is being transferred between the server and workstation.

If programs run more slowly on the workstation, they do so because they are using data from the server and must constantly access it. Picture this transaction as starting in a large room in the workstation. There is lots of room to work, but when you need to get the data, you have to open a door, run down a long narrow hallway, grab the data with a bucket, run all the way back, and again open the door on your system. How quickly you can make the trip depends on the speed at which you can run and what kind of door is at each end of the hallway.

Another speed factor is the amount you can carry as you run down the hall. The size of the bucket varies with the network, but in most cases, the data is moved quickly because you can run quickly, not because you have big buckets. And yes, there are other runners standing at the same doorway at the server end of the hall. The server can open only one door at a time. You may have to run as hard as you can to get to the door, but if others got there first, you'll have to wait in line.

To use this analogy in an example, when you first initiate a connection to the network, your system sends the runner across the network wire. In the bucket is your first message: You want to be recognized by (*log on*) the system. The runner knocks on the server door or, if other users have sent runners, waits in line to knock. The server door opens and the server reads the data in the bucket—in this case, a logon request. That request is then processed by the server. The server responds by placing data in the bucket and sending the runner back to your system with the prompt Name. Your system reads the server's data bucket asking your logon name and places the information on your screen. When you type the response, the runner begins the trip back down the wire to deliver the response data.

1

Each time you load a program file, use a data file, or send data to a network printer, this transaction occurs. The complications occur because other users are also sending runners down the same wire to knock on the server's door. Each bucket requires a response from the server before the next bucket can be read and processed. All this data running back and forth creates the network *traffic*.

Distributing the Workload

While there are many variables to consider in a small network, one of the first decisions is how to distribute the workload. While a small network need not set aside a powerful system as a server, more powerful networks require dedicated servers.

Dedicated Servers

To start with the most powerful, but most expensive, arrangement, consider a LAN with a *dedicated server*. This means a network with a separate system set aside to do nothing but handle the traffic and other tasks for the LAN. This arrangement is essential with networks containing more than ten workstations. The server can be optimized with a large hard disk and lots of memory and have a fast processor. There are a number of companies that sell desktop systems designed to handle server duties, and these systems come at a premium price, some over $10,000. That high price may be worth it if the server might be handling a hundred or more workstations. On the other hand, a properly configured, fast desktop system can serve a small network quite well.

Nondedicated Servers

Moving down the scale, more within the range of the small network, are the nondedicated and peer-to-peer systems. The *nondedicated server* is a system functioning both as a network host and a workstation. The software allows the system to perform two functions at one time: when network requests come in, the software handles that request, and when the user sitting in front of the system wants to print a document, the software handles that request as well.

What if both requests are made at the same time or if the network request requires a lot of processing time? How well the nondedicated server handles those situations depends on how powerful the system is and how the priority ratio has been set.

Dual Purpose Requires Power

If the nondedicated system is very powerful, the user may not notice much delay in the current application. For example, for the few fractions of a second the system turns its attention to the network, the local user may notice that the results of each keypress are not displayed on the screen. When the system can return to the local program, those keystrokes are caught up on the screen and the program continues. If the system is not as powerful, the user may have to pause until the screen catches up with the last keystrokes typed.

Setting the Priority Ratio

The *priority ratio* is usually set when the network is installed. A typical ratio of 50/50 means that the processor time is shared equally, while a ratio of 80/20 means that more processing time is devoted to the network requests. The ratio can usually be changed to fine-tune the system. If this system is used for a text-based word processor and network traffic is heavy, the 80/20 ratio may work. If more demanding applications are run locally and the network requests are intermittent, the 50/50 ratio might work. In the worst case, you might have to turn the system into a dedicated server.

Sharing Tasks with Peer-to-Peer Networks

Another alternative to the nondedicated server is for each system to function both as a server and as a workstation. This *peer-to-peer networking* is very popular for small networks because each computer system can share resources such as disk space and printers with each other computer on the network. Peer-to-peer networks can be a very cost-effective way to make use of limited resources.

For example, each of three peer-to-peer systems could have a specific printer. One system might have a laser printer, and a second could have a dot matrix with 14-inch-wide paper. Anyone on the network could send printing to the system with the laser printer attached just as anyone could send printing for wide paper to the second system. The users with the printers attached would be able to use their systems normally. The difference would be that the printer would begin printing when they did not expect it to print.

Deciding on the best approach depends on your current resources, budget, and anticipated network traffic. The dedicated system ties up a computer, making it the more expensive system. The nondedicated server makes one system the host but keeps it available for other work. The peer-to-peer system spreads the responsibilities out across the network but may prove to be the most complicated of all the networks to design and use. Chapter 5 expands on these considerations when designing your network.

From the User's Perspective

As with any change to a computer system, the users need to know how that change affects them and how to use the new system. While user training is covered in Chapters 7 and 8, this section summarizes how the network appears to the user from DOS. If the workstations use a menu system, the users may see only that the network has allowed more menu selections.

From DOS, the network connections appear as additional drives and printer ports. For example, the user has a local drive C and one dot matrix printer, attached to the printer port, LPT1. Once the network is added, the user might have drive G for the system-wide mailing list database, drive H for more disk space to store data and programs, and drive M for an E-mail system. To use these areas of the file server, the user enters the drive letter and colon at any DOS prompt.

To print something on the network laser printer located down the hall, the user need only send the output to LPT2 instead of LTP1, the local printer. The data prints quickly because the network takes the input from the user's program and holds it until the printer is ready. The user can then change to another task.

Those drive designations are based entirely on the network design. Selecting LPT2 for the network printer also makes sense for the users. Not only can the designer choose the drives to represent areas on the server, the users can also be restricted to specific areas and specific functions. For example, a user might be able to use drive G only to print mailing labels. With restricted access, that user could not make any changes to the data files, including updating records or deleting files. A chart showing the user's system could look like the one illustrated in Figure 1-4.

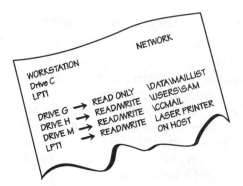

A sketch of a
user's network
access
Figure 1-4.

"Need a Network?" Checklist

This is a two-pass checklist. Complete the questions now as part of your assessment. Additional comments about each question are provided after the questions. But since there are no hard and fast rules, return to this checklist *after* you have read the rest of the book and see if your responses remain the same. (You may also notice that this is a good planning document if you decide to install a network.)

1. List the resources you need to share among users:

   a. Printers:

   b. Disk space:

   c. Fax boards:

1

d. Modems:

e. CD-ROM drives:

f. Other:

2. Do users frequently exchange disks containing data files?

3. Do users need to use the same data files?

4. Would you like to pass messages to each other without walking to each office or desk?

5. Do you have a system powerful enough (at least a 286) to function as the main server for printing and file sharing? If not, will you buy one?

6. Are the workstations on the same floor, with a suspended ceiling to run the network cables?

7. Can you afford to spend from $200 to $400 per workstation?

8. Do you have the extra time required to design and manage the network?

9. Are you ready to handle the new problems created by the network?

10. Do you have someone who can provide help when you need it?

Remember, this is not a test. You cannot send it to Osborne/ McGraw-Hill to see if you have earned a passing score. It is just a way to help you think about the network. The more "Yes" answers you have to these questions, the more likely it is that you can benefit from a network. Here are some additional considerations for each question.

1. If you just want to share a printer or two, there are a number of products dedicated to that task. Don't think you have to install a network just so everyone can use the one laser printer in the office. Adding a network just to provide more disk storage for each user is also *not* cost effective. Buy everyone an additional or larger hard disk instead. If you want to share several of the resources in this list, a network begins to make sense.

2. If your office uses common files such as a standard rejection letter, being able to read that file from the server keeps the letter consistent. Once the letter is changed on the server, everyone immediately begins to use the updated letter.

3. If you have answered yes to this question, a network is essential. Typically this problem occurs when more than one person begins using a specific database. For example, if the sales accounts are now being entered by two people, those records must be added to the main database. Keep in mind that this requires special software for a network. You can't easily copy the single user's database to the server and expect everyone to be able to use it.

4. Sending electronic mail (E-mail) to other users is not usually a primary reason for getting a small network. Once a network is installed, or as part of the justification for getting the network, E-mail is very handy. On the other hand, if you constantly miss each other on the phone or must complete a log of pink "while you were out" slips, a LAN E-mail system may weigh heavily in the decision.

5. Even with the smallest of networks, you'll need at least one system to handle the main network chores. You can't expect to build a network on five-year-old computers. The older systems might be acceptable as workstations.

6. With drop ceilings, you can poke your head up into the tiles and toss the cable. If yours is an older building with high ceilings and concrete walls, you'll have more work (and expense) ahead. Even a

small network can become a major project when the cable is difficult to install.

7. Even with the cheapest of networks, you have to budget at least $200 per workstation on the network. This includes the network card and the software.

8. If you are already running on overdrive, adding a network will put you over the edge. While the network may save time in the long run, you'll have to commit to more hours at first to save hours later. Don't even think about a network if you are in the middle of a major project within the office. A network is rarely an emergency. If it is, pay someone else to do everything but the design.

9. Networks add another level of complexity to your life. If you have mastered the essence of desktop computers, you'll be starting over on the learning curve when you install a network.

10. Don't even consider installing a network yourself unless you have lined up someone to help if you need it. It may be someone you have to pay. In fact, it should be someone you have to pay. You'll need that person's experience in a hurry if you need help.

Summary

This chapter has introduced you to the basics of a network. It provided the definition of a network, defined some terms, and put you to work reviewing the design of existing networks and thinking about your network. Here is what you have discovered:

✦ Computers are connected to create a network that shares resources such as printers, disk space, data files, and other devices.

✦ Desktop computers represent freedom from the mainframe because the computer system is under individual control.

✦ Networks range in size from two systems, side by side, connected through their serial ports to multiple workstations and servers connected around the world.

✦ Local area networks (LANs) may have one system serving as the central host, or the hosting job may be shared among the connected computers.

✦ Design, installation, supervision, and maintenance are all different parts of getting, and keeping, the network running.

✦ All the reasons for getting a network may not be obvious now but may become more apparent after the network is functional.

CHAPTER

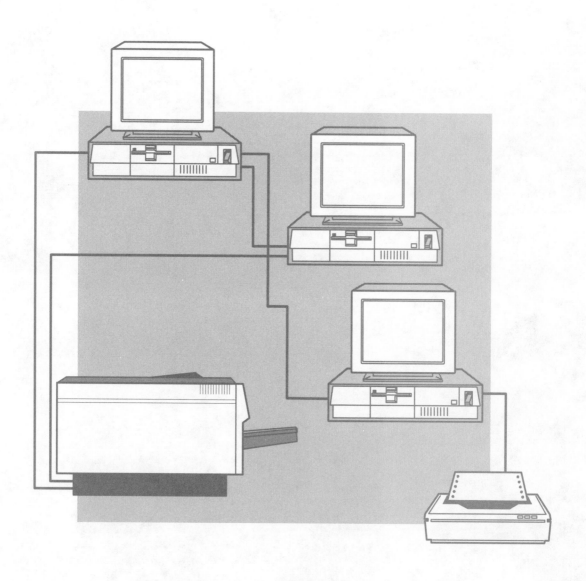

2

ADVANTAGES AND DISADVANTAGES OF NETWORKED COMPUTERS

Installing a network can increase the usefulness of desktop computers in the workplace. This chapter covers the reasons you might want a network as well as the potential problems a network can introduce. A checklist helps you decide if you are ready and willing to install and manage a network.

Connecting computers adds a whole new level of complexity to your computer use. Before you make the decision to install a network, you need to know what you, and your users, might gain. You also need to know the disadvantages. This chapter provides a number of reasons to make the network connection, including sharing printers, disk space, and program and data files and using E-mail.

The dark side of networking is also exposed, including additional expenses, increased complexity, and the extra time required to supervise the network. Other factors to consider are also covered, including critical task usage, backups, and network software.

Tips and suggestions are provided throughout this chapter to deal with possible problems, reduce the disadvantages, or just to look at using the LAN in a new way. Use the "Analysis Guide" to create your own checklist of advantages and disadvantages of installing the network.

Sharing Resources

Networks allow workstations to use parts of other desktop computers, typically hard drives and printers. With a single-server network, all those parts (resources) are attached to one desktop system, the server. All the other workstations just "hang on" to the server's resources. Other network types, such as peer-to-peer, allow each system to share part of itself on the network.

The type of network you select will depend on the location of these resources and how willing you are to group these resources or leave them dispersed. The resource examples provided in the next sections do not necessarily depend on the physical location of the resource.

This first section covers physical resources such as printers, drives, modems, fax boards, and CD-ROM drives. The next sections discuss using files as resources. While these are also potential network resources, they represent a very different level of complexity. Each of these resources is also illustrated in Chapter 5, which covers network planning.

Accessing Printers

One of the most common reasons to network is to allow everyone to use one printer. Typically, that printer is a laser printer attached to the server. As users on the network send jobs to that printer, the pages pile up until someone retrieves the stack and distributes the printouts.

For users, that network printer can appear as LPT2 on their system. To send the print data to the network printer instead of the local printer, the users select LPT2 within the software. The network printer may also be the only printer the users have. The users get hard copy by sending the material to be printed to the network printer and then walking to that printer to pick up the pages.

That little walk suggests one of the disadvantages of networking printers. While the printer may produce nice-looking output, it takes productive time away from the users as they stroll down the hall to retrieve the hard copy. Also keep in mind that unless a laser printer is rated for heavy use, you may find you wear out the printer quickly. You then have to buy another to replace it.

Another disadvantage of sharing one printer is the use of special paper, typically printed letterhead. One reason to use the laser printer is to print on company letterhead. To use letterhead, you have to

1. Make sure no one else is printing.
2. Put the letterhead paper in.
3. Run back to your office.
4. Send the document to the printer.
5. Run back to the printer.
6. Retrieve the printed letterhead.
7. Remove any extra letterhead sheets.
8. Let everyone know they can print again.

Only if the users are all within visual and voice range does this make sense. Otherwise the user has to run up and down the hall yelling instructions to the other users.

If you have not purchased the laser printer to share on the network, you should consider a multibin printer. These printers contain two or more paper stacks. If your software supports this type of printer, you can select the proper bin, in this case the stack of letterhead paper. With a multibin printer, there is no need to go through the steps just outlined.

TIP: The cost/benefit ratio is an important consideration when you decide where to locate printers. One good measure might be the size of the print jobs and how frequently the users need to print. To take the letterhead example, it may be much less expensive and save time to give each user an inkjet printer. While these types of printers produce laser-quality output, they are very inexpensive (less than $400) and extremely quiet. The slower printing speed will not be important for small but frequent print jobs.

The network printer may be a fast dot matrix printer with wide paper. This could be helpful for those occasional spreadsheets that just won't fit on normal-sized paper. Everyone can have access through the server.

Sharing Hard Drive Space

Hard drive space becomes more precious with newer programs. Just when you thought it was safe to purchase 40MB hard drives, some programs now require 10MB of disk space when loaded. Older systems may have 20MB drives, or they might not have hard drives at all.

A network provides more hard disk storage for everyone attached. In most cases, the network supervisor creates areas on the server assigned only to that user. The user can treat that hard disk as an additional drive and use it just as though it were located in the workstation. Depending on the network software, you may be able to limit the maximum size for each user.

Sharing hard drive space is also more efficient. Users who need lots of space, get it. Users who don't generate many new files don't take up much space. This contrasts with workstations all configured with 80MB hard drives. Some users run out of space quickly and some may not use even one fourth of the capacity. The network hard disk storage provides the economy of scale and distribution as needed. This also provides a higher level of security if program and data access are an issue on the network.

Sharing hard drive space on a server does have its disadvantages; the most obvious is having "all the eggs in one basket." If everyone has saved critical data on one hard drive and the drive fails, all the data is lost unless proper backups exist.

Actual access time may be an advantage or a disadvantage. Server storage may also be slower or faster than a local drive, depending on the network transmission speeds, traffic, and older hard drive access speeds. With an older drive, network access may actually be faster than using the local hard drive.

Sharing Modems and Phone Lines

Sharing hard drive space and printers is considered an essential part of most network systems. Within the past few years, special network versions of software have allowed users to share modems, fax boards, and CD-ROM drives. While this does require additional software, the cost savings may be substantial when averaged out by the number of users on the network.

For example, Procomm Plus LAN from Datastorm provides every user with access to a modem and a phone line somewhere on the network. While the cost of a 2400-baud modem (under $100) is not prohibitive, tying up the voice line or adding a second phone line to the user's office may be. A high-speed modem, 9600 baud or greater, is also high priced, $500 or more. Sharing this expense over the network may help justify the higher performance gain.

As with all resources, use of LAN-based communications depends on the anticipated need. If eight users rely on an outside E-mail service and check their mail four times a day, the network may need a communications server with two or more modems. If there are only three users who use outside research services via modem, and only occasionally, a modem located in one workstation may be acceptable.

Replacing Fax Machines

Businesses have become obsessed with sending information by fax, in part because data transmission is so easy. Anyone can dial a phone. Anyone can place a sheet of paper in the machine. Anyone can read an incoming fax printout.

This capability has been extended to the desktop computer. Modems have now become modem/fax boards. Any LAN user can send a fax from a workstation. The fax software translates the computer data file into the format required for a fax, dials the phone number, and sends the message to a standard fax machine. Each user on the network has a fax account. Incoming fax pages can be displayed on the user's screen or printed to most printers. Products like Intel's NET SatisFAXtion Software bring those capabilities to the network.

The rationale for having one fax board with LAN-based software closely matches the reasons advanced for a modem. In fact, some of the more advanced boards can accept an incoming call from either a fax or a modem and switch the signal to the software to handle the call.

If your fax machine is in high demand, the line of people waiting to use the machine represents lost productivity. A LAN-based fax server may pay for itself in increased employee productivity.

The major disadvantage of sending a fax through the computer network is that the image must be routed through the system. In many cases, this is not an issue. If the work is created on the computer, whether graphics or text based, the fax software can translate that image into the fax signal. If the original is on paper, it must be read with a page scanner before it can be transmitted through the computer. The cost of a page scanner can easily be twice the expense of a standard fax machine.

Another disadvantage of incoming electronic fax is distribution. Of course, this is also a problem with a paper-based fax system. Most fax system software routes the fax data to the fax administrator on the network. This individual must then read the cover sheet to put the fax in the appropriate user's fax mailbox. A well-tended incoming fax file system can easily beat the benign neglect afforded many paper-based fax machines.

This disadvantage is being removed through the use of more sophisticated software. These systems use caller ID and network addresses to route the fax transmissions. This is effective only when the fax transmissions are from LAN to LAN, though, because a paper-based fax machine cannot use the electronic address for a user on the LAN.

The need to transmit fax messages is based on less sophisticated use of a paper-based fax machine on the other end of the line. Once E-mail (covered in the section "Using E-mail" later in this chapter) becomes more popular, the need for fax machines will diminish. With a workstation at both ends of the transmission, the message need not be rendered on paper.

Sharing CD-ROM Drives

CD-ROM is another technology that has become more popular within the past few years. The same technology used with music CDs has been applied to computer data storage. One CD-ROM (compact disk/read-only memory) can hold up to 650MB of information. Because this device is read-only, it is a reference tool, not a data storage resource.

For example, one disk can contain an entire encyclopedia including 33,000 articles, hundreds of color illustrations and photos, and sounds of musical instruments, animals, and speeches. Another popular CD-ROM contains a complete dictionary, a library desk reference, a dictionary of 20th century history, hundreds of legal forms, a book about writing, a spelling checker, a book of quotations, and more. Other CD-ROM titles include legal materials, a history of stock quotations, two years' worth of 20 different magazines, and some very interactive educational programs.

The costs for a CD-ROM range from $50 and up, with many useful titles costing less than $200. Some CD-ROM drives cost less than $500. On an individual computer, the drive becomes an additional drive. If the system has drives C and D as the hard drive, the CD-ROM drive automatically becomes drive E.

When you use CD-ROMs on the network, the data accessibility is multiplied by the number of users. A product such as CD Connection from CBIS provides access to one or more CD-ROM drives from anywhere in the network. The costs of providing this kind of reference on the network may extend beyond the disk and the drive. To provide the quickest access to the data, CBIS has designed the CD software to run on a dedicated desktop system with lots of memory, 8MB minimum. Up to 21 drives can be included in this dedicated system. The cost of the system, memory, and network card must be included with the cost of the CD-ROM drive and disk.

Other network software supports CD-ROM drives as network resources. For example, LANtastic can use a local CD-ROM as though it were just another hard drive. While the small network is unlikely to require a dedicated CD-ROM server, a CD-ROM drive may present a new way for users to benefit from the network.

Two cautions need to be stated here. As with any application, make sure the material users need to share across the network is available on

CD-ROM. A $3000 investment in a system and drive makes little sense if the material is not yet on CD-ROM. On the other hand, more and more material is being offered on CD-ROM. You can add the CD-ROM server later if you find that users can benefit from the access.

The other caution relates to copyright of the material on the CD-ROM, for both reuse and multiple access. These issues are very unclear, and each CD-ROM distributor handles them differently. Some say that you can clip and reuse anything on the CD-ROM as long as credit is given within the second use (your document). Others maintain that all copyrights apply and you can not reuse the material in any way.

Most CD-ROMs currently being distributed assume a single user at one time. With the multiplication of users on the network, more than one user can access the data at once. Check the copyright notice carefully on any CD-ROM you purchase to understand the publisher's position on reuse of the material and multiple access.

Files as Resources

Since everyone on the network can potentially access the same space on the server's hard disk, everyone can use the same files. This is called *file sharing*. File sharing can be broken down into file exchange and data sharing. Each type of file you use creates problems, many of which you can anticipate in your network design. Remember that you determine who uses each area on the server.

Exchanging Files

Two-way file exchanges can also be one-way. These one-way exchanges are called *file libraries*. Once the user loads the file into his or her application at the workstation, changes to the file are not kept on the server. The changes become part of the user's saved files. Any users with access to that open area of the file server can, at a minimum, load the file into their system.

File Library

A file library is an area on the file server hard disk that is designated as a read-only area by the supervisor. For example, a group leader could maintain a library of 15 standard form letters to be used with most correspondence. The leader can both save and load files from the library directory. Each of the correspondence clerks can access that library only to read the files into his or her word processor. They then make the changes to personalize the letter. They can't save the changed file back to the file server, although they can save it anywhere else they have write access, including their local hard drive.

The essential point of the file library is the one-way flow of data. If someone other than the group leader were to save a changed version to the library, the change would ripple down for each user loading that file later. If more than one person could save files to that location, they would need to work out a system for who is allowed to change files and when.

Submitting Drafts and Finals

Work group software is another new product based on LAN connectivity. This software typically provides E-mail, file grouping, version tracking, project management, and more, in one package. The same concepts can be applied in a small network setting without relying on a specific work group program. The difference is that the group decides how to use what they have.

If you do not use special work group software, you must design a useful file-naming convention. As a common example of why this is needed, consider the situation of two people who work on the document at the same time and return their versions of the update. Someone then has to go through both versions and reconcile the differences.

One method of naming files is to start project filenames with a four-character designation. After that, two numbers indicate the draft version, and the final two characters represent the author. The first version of a project file about widgets created by Eric Daniels might be named WIDG01ED.DOC. When Mary Allison continues the work, she reads the WIDG01ED.DOC file, makes changes, and saves the file as WIDG01MA.DOC. Once the version has been viewed by everyone in the group, the version number increases to 02.

Sharing Data

Data sharing allows multiple users to access the same file at the same time and make changes. This type of sharing typically applies to database files, with users changing individual records. Sequential changes to the data are relatively easy. Simultaneous changes require special LAN database software. The following explanation assumes that you understand basic database concepts.

Making Sequential Changes

Unlike the file exchange where files are read-only or where new versions are created with each change, some data files need to be changed by a number of users. In the single-user environment, the file resides on the local disk and the user makes changes as necessary. In the network environment, this single-user program is not able to make changes to different parts of the file at the same time.

However, if the users can wait their turns, the program and data file or files can be moved to the network. This works with most non-network software because once the file is opened by one user, no one can access that file until the file is closed. This is similar to borrowing a book from the library—no one can read the book while someone else has it checked out.

If you do move this type of data file to the network, test the process on a backup copy of the file. The non-network-aware program may not perform as expected and may corrupt the data instead of locking users out. Make sure you have a legitimate copy of the single-user software for each individual using the network-resident version, as explained in the "Network Software" section later in this chapter.

Making Simultaneous Changes

The ultimate file resource level allows simultaneous changes to records in a data file. For example, the personnel department may maintain a database of all 700 employees. Each employee record contains basic ID fields as well as job changes and pay grades. Each of the five users in the department is responsible for different areas of the employee record.

While one user is updating the health insurance portion of an employee record, another may need to make a change to someone else's job status. Only if the database software has been designed to run on a LAN can the employee database be accessed by two different users. If both users attempt to make changes to the same employee's record, one of the users is prompted by the software to either wait or locate another record.

2

While this simultaneous use of data files represents the best of data sharing, it is also the most complicated. A number of basic database programs are now sold in LAN versions. For example, PC-File 6.5 LAN allows file sharing across a network. More complicated database applications on a LAN, such as dBASE IV, require a programmer to design and write code for the project.

LAN-based Activities

The LAN connection provides new ways of using desktop computers. In addition to the sharing of resources and files, special network software provides message exchange and scheduling. These software tools provide a path to a nearly paperless office. With some creativity, the LAN becomes the foundation for network-based work groups.

Using E-mail

Electronic mail (E-mail) represents the transmission of data packages from one person to another person or group of people. These data packages may be text messages or a collection of items including a text message and various files. The transmission starts and ends on a computer. This definition applies to messages sent over phone lines to other information services, such as CompuServe, as well as messages routed within your local network.

Some network software includes a very basic form of mail, usually added to help administrative functions. For example, the SEND command in a common LAN program can be used to send a one-line message to one or all users. This would be essential if, for some reason, the server had to be taken down (turned off). The supervisor could send a message to all users that the network would be shut down at a specific time. The users could then log themselves off of the network.

More successful and useful E-mail programs provide a wide variety of features. cc:Mail from Lotus is a top-selling package. This program allows you to create messages and attach files to those messages. When you receive messages, you can store them on a local drive or archive them to floppy disk. All messages are encrypted so no one but the sender and recipient can read the message. E-mail also allows an audit trail of messages and group mailing-list addresses.

Electronic mail offers the advantage of holding mail until the recipient is available. The disadvantage is that the recipient must run the mail program before he or she can read the mail. If you send an urgent message, it will be delayed until the next time the recipient chooses to run the E-mail program. Some E-mail programs, though, can alert users that a message has been sent to their E-mail box even while they are running other applications.

Few organizations would set up a small LAN just to provide E-mail for the users. As the system designer, you may want to consider installing an E-mail program once the LAN is stable. Once users become familiar with E-mail and see it as a new and important channel of communication, they'll begin using it consistently.

Scheduling Multiple Appointments

Appointment books have also moved into the realm of networking. Network scheduling software keeps a database of everyone's appointment schedule. The details of any one schedule are available only to designated users. For example, a secretary can have access to his or her boss's schedule. Certain blocks of time can be left open for appointments. Only the secretary and the boss can see and change the schedule.

Open time in individual calendars can be used to schedule meetings. The software can check each schedule to find a common opening and, once it is found, update everyone's schedule with the meeting details. Regularly scheduled meetings can automatically be entered in everyone's schedule.

NOTE: There are mixed feelings about scheduling software. Some users report that they feel "micromanaged" with this software. They never know when someone else will claim their time. Other work groups claim they can't live without scheduling software. These users report that the trick is to block out a reasonable amount of time for yourself and then let the system work around those blocks.

2

Creating a Paperless Office

While a paperless office may still be a few years away, careful design of a LAN and effective use of E-mail can reduce the amount of paper floating through offices. An E-mail program that allows message storage and an organized approach for storing those messages is essential.

For example, the memo author can send a memo to one individual or a preset group of users. When each individual signs on, the memo is in his or her incoming E-mail. The author can even receive a message from the mail system confirming when each recipient reads the memo.

TIP: If you have trouble with users checking their mail, send a paper message that just starts the memo. Then indicate that the remainder of the memo is sitting in their E-mailboxes. They'll have to use the E-mail program to get the details. An upcoming office party announcement would be a good motivational memo.

Facilitating Group Work

As mentioned, a LAN can facilitate group interaction and cooperation for projects. Software specifically developed for this has been labeled "groupware." Some types, as discussed previously, include scheduling, E-mail, file grouping, version tracking, and project management. Other types of groupware features may exist in programs you already use. For example, there may be a way for several users to make changes in a text document. The final version is created only after everyone has read and approved the changes.

The advantages of using a LAN for group projects should not be overlooked. Just using E-mail prevents the constant game of telephone tag. When ideas are shared via E-mail, they will have been thought out enough to be put into writing. Being able to save communications between team members can provide an activity trail and history of the project.

Remember that groupware is more a concept than one piece of software. It is up to the users, and the network supervisor, to put together the system that helps them accomplish their project.

The Other Side of LANs

The previous examples have provided reasons why you might want to install a LAN. Some topics did mention a disadvantage or two, but the full story hasn't been told until you confront the reasons why you *don't* want to install a LAN.

Increasing Complexity

In an informal survey, a number of LAN administrators were asked what they wish they had known before they installed the network. They all wished they had known how long the installation would take. One administrator offered this advice: "Estimate the time. Double it and double it again. You might be close."

While this is not an effort to talk you out of installing a LAN, it is an attempt to prepare you for the inevitable problems. The first and foremost is the increased complexity. Each of your desktop computers may have been fine tuned. The software is completely installed, the memory conflicts resolved, and the performance optimized to the user's satisfaction. When the LAN is installed, all this may go out the window.

More "Things" to Break

Consider just the new parts added to make the physical connections. Each system on the network will contain a network board. As covered in more detail in Chapter 6, you may have to deal with interrupt settings, dip switches, and the physical location of the board in the system. Each of these variables represents something that can go wrong. The board itself may also not work or "go bad."

Each section of cable, from one connection to the next, represents something else that can fail. The connector may not be crimped properly on the cable, the connection may not be making good contact with the plug, or sometime later the cable may be accidentally cut.

The biggest thing to "break" is the server. Whether you have a dedicated or nondedicated server, as soon as other users begin to depend on the resources provided by that system, it becomes more important. A corollary of Murphy's Law states, "The more everyone depends on the server, the more likely it will fail."

Each resource on the network, including hard drives, printers, modems, fax boards, CD-ROMs, and other devices, represents something breakable. Each of these elements adds to the complexity of the system and provides something else to maintain.

Program and Memory Conflicts

The network connection requires each workstation to load and run programs in memory. Depending on the network, this memory use may range from as little as 12K to as much as 100K. Without the use of sophisticated memory-handling software, that space is taken from the 640K of memory. If, for example, the application programs require 540K to run and only 500K remain after the network software is loaded, the workstation can either connect to the network or run the application, but it can't do both—hardly an effective way to run a network.

Because the network software must be present at all times to maintain the connection, it is co-managing the applications along with the operating system. While the network software companies can develop and test their software while running various operating systems, there are just too many applications to test completely. It is quite possible that the application software may conflict with the network software. The conflict may occur with a particular version of the operating system combined with a particular version of the applications program.

Keep in mind that newer operating systems and environments like Windows are not limited as much by memory. Also, because networks are being used on more systems, the program designers try to anticipate problems related to network use. The section "Network Software" later in this chapter also provides some insights on this issue.

Mission-critical Activities

Part of your design will include the company-wide tasks to be transferred to the network. These activities might include the accounting system, the employee records, the inventory, or any number of tasks. Moving these to the network means that where the data was once located on one system, it now rests effectively in everyone's system, or it is at least accessible to anyone you choose.

If your company depends on one or more tasks as the main source of revenue, these are "mission-critical" tasks. For example, if your company produces customized coupon billing booklets for a loan company, your mission-critical task is the calculation and printing of those booklets. If your accounting system goes down for a day or two, someone will have to do some extra work, but the company can survive. If your coupon system goes down, you are losing money every minute it is down. If you are using the system 24 hours a day, seven days a week, you can never recover the lost time. That is a critical loss to the company.

LAN Stability: How Trustworthy?

Consider very carefully how quickly you want to trust those kinds of tasks to the network. If you are installing a LAN to allow more than one user to access a program, make sure you leave plenty of overlap between the transfer from a single- to a multiple-user system. As soon as you relegate a mission-critical task to the LAN, the performance takes on a whole new importance. While the LAN may have started as a convenience, it soon becomes a necessity.

Just as you'll make the transition to the LAN from each workstation slowly, the transition to the LAN-based tasks should also be carefully planned. You should consider the following:

✦ How long does the network remain stable?

✦ What kind of backup do you have?

✦ How quickly can you get help with repairs?

A network that crashes once a week and takes a day to recover is not a candidate for serious applications until those problems are resolved. Remember, too, that as you increase the load by adding new tasks, you are likely to discover new problems. Save yourself some headaches and leave yourself with a way out if necessary.

Prepare for the Worst

You don't requisition a fire extinguisher the first time you smell smoke. An effective LAN manager prepares for the worst. Chapter 8 covers many of the disaster-planning issues, but you'll need to consider this additional task as one of the disadvantages of installing a network.

You'll need to assume that the server is destroyed by a fire and plan how your business would recover. What happens if five workstations are stolen? Imagine all the data on the file server being erased and plan for that disaster. What happens if the network guru leaves for another job? All these, and more, become time-consuming responsibilities, magnified by the importance of the data on the network.

Creating and Solving Maintenance Problems

Regular maintenance is both an advantage and a disadvantage on a LAN. The LAN can provide a timely way to back up critical files. As mentioned, it also provides more pieces of the puzzle to handle.

Backing up the Server

If you choose to have all of your eggs in one basket (files on the server), you must plan to back up those files on a regular basis. If you have a small LAN with several workstations and a nondedicated server, you need to back up daily. If you have a slightly larger LAN with seven workstations and a dedicated server, you also need to back up daily.

You should perform a daily backup regardless of the size of your system. What may differ is the method. On a smaller system, you may find a fast backup program that will copy the contents of an 80MB hard disk to 30 HD (high density) floppy disks in 20 minutes. You'll do this complete backup once a week. In between, you'll do an incremental backup, copying only files that have changed since the last backup. That step may take only five minutes.

If the server is larger or if many files change daily, you may want to consider a tape drive. A tape drive is used to copy the contents of a hard disk in one pass. For larger hard disks, 100MB and beyond, a backup tape system is necessary because of the long time that would be required if floppy disks were used. Chapter 8 describes tape drives and backup methods in more detail.

Performing User Backup

Users are notoriously bad about backing up data. They see backing up files as a time-consuming task with no payoff, so they usually don't do it. You may choose to design the network so that all users save all files on the server. Since the server is backed up daily, the job of safeguarding the work done in the office has been assigned to the LAN.

If the workstations do not have hard drives, this backup plan works by default. If the local systems do have hard drives, the users need to understand that unless they do their own backup, the only files being backed up are those they keep on the server.

As the data kept on local hard drives becomes more important to the company, the use of the LAN to safeguard this data becomes more critical. This factor alone may be enough reason to install a LAN and design the system so that the critical data rests on the file server. As an alternative, backup scheduling software can be installed on the workstations to back up each user's hard disk to the file server. Of course, the user must remember to leave the system on in the evening for the backup program to work.

Providing Equipment Backup

Larger LAN installations prepare for the inevitable hardware failure by maintaining hardware backups as well. This means that they keep new or rebuilt equipment ready to replace anything that goes awry. For example, when a user reports a problem with a computer, the support technician can copy the user's hard disk files to the network, replace the entire system with a new system, and then restore the files from the network. Downtime can be as little as 30 minutes.

A smaller installation may not have the luxury of having a spare part for everything in the network. If the equipment has been purchased over the years, the parts may not be very interchangeable. Even the smallest network should have a plan for hardware failure.

NOTE: Equipment backup may mean that a user who depends on his or her computer less may temporarily lose the computer to a user with more computer tasks. Server backup may be an alternate server normally used as a workstation.

2

Network Software

There are both practical and legal issues related to the use of software on a network. These issues, as well as providing a new type of system support, create additional advantages and disadvantages.

Evaluating Single User vs. Network Software

Before networks became popular, software was sold to run on one computer at a time. The programs were designed to load into memory and handle the input from one individual. With the advent of LAN software, this older type of software is now referred to as "single-user" software.

LAN-based software is designed to be loaded by a specified number of users. While each copy is loaded and runs from the workstations, those local copies are aware of the network and can save files on the network and use network printers. The programs also need to handle any conflicts on the network by file sharing or overwriting.

A major advantage of storing one copy of the application on the server is to save space on the local drives. Since many programs must be configured to the individual computer and workstations on the network may not match, the LAN software should be able to provide for user configuration files.

For example, Microsoft Word for Windows handles the problem of multiple copies easily. The SETUP program allows the network administrator to copy all program files to the server. Each user then installs just the configuration files on his or her local system. The main files remain on the server. Even though the program is easily networkable, the software license does state that you must have legal copies for the maximum number of possible users.

Some single-user programs will run on networks with varying degrees of success. Some allow multiple workstation loads, can handle the network drives for file storage, and can use network printers. Others may load from the server but refuse to see the network drives. Some single-user programs can be copied to the server but refuse to load and run, or they may load but run with frequent errors. A few single-user programs are "network aware" and halt immediately when they detect that they are running from a network with the warning "Not a network version" or a similar message.

Contact the software companies to see if a LAN version exists. If not, ask if there are any known problems with using the single-user version on a LAN.

LAN Software Use Restrictions

In general, software programs are sold to be used by one person at a time on one computer. Regardless of the success of running a single-user version on the network, most software licenses insist that a legal copy of the program exist for all users and potential users on a network. For example, one copy can be installed on the network, but for every user on the network, a copy of the program and manuals must have been purchased and exist at the work site.

The count can become rather vague:

+ Does this count apply to every workstation attached to the network?

+ Do six workstations require six copies?

+ What if only two people ever use the program at the same time? Can you just buy two copies in this situation?

+ What happens if a third user tries to load the program?

LAN versions of the software use several approaches. One allows a specific number of users and others allow an unlimited number of users but require that the LAN administrator monitor the number of users. Other vendors provide site licenses or even server-based licenses. Vendors have several variations on the LAN-based theme.

The LAN software package should state the number of users allowed by the license. For example, Procomm Plus LAN, mentioned in the

"Sharing Modems and Phone Lines" section of this chapter, is licensed for five users. The CD Connection and Intel's NET SatisFAXtion are not limited to the number of users. Because these two packages require the shared use of a hardware resource, they are limited to the number of users with access to that equipment.

These limits may be "hard wired" into the software or may be based on the honor system. With a hard-wired five-user program, the software refuses to allow the sixth workstation to load the software until one of the other five quits the program. With others, especially larger packages, the company depends on the system administrator to monitor the number of active users. If the number of users exceeds the license number, the administrator is expected to purchase additional user licenses. While monitoring the number of users may not seem difficult to the small network administrator, planning for growth requires this consideration.

Some site- or server-based licenses are open-ended. The company purchases an unlimited number of copies to be used within the company or from one server. These licenses are usually very expensive and not applicable to the small network.

In many cases, purchasing the LAN version of the software is cheaper than purchasing individual copies. In most cases, though, the software package includes only one copy of the manual. Some companies offer registered users copies of the manual for modest prices. The Procomm Plus LAN is an exception. With the license for five users comes five complete sets of manuals.

For the administrator of a smaller network, the purchase of the LAN version may or may not be more economical. Some companies provide a set number of user licenses, typically starting with 5 and jumping to 10 or 20 users. If you have 3 or 7 users, you'll have to pay for those extra users even though you don't need them. Of course, if your network grows, you'll immediately be ready for the extra workstation connections.

Part of this consideration should be the potential problems in trying to run a single-user version on the LAN. A possible solution is to run each legal copy on the individual workstation and use the network for data files and printer sharing.

Providing System Support

Providing support for programs used on the LAN does present an advantage. The most obvious is that all the users are on the same version of the software. Any time you want to upgrade, everyone makes the jump when you install the newer version over the old.

Not as common in smaller networks is remote LAN support software. A support person and user can both use a program to allow the support person to view and work with the user's system as though sitting in front of it. During the course of the call, the user can demonstrate the steps leading to the problem. The support person can watch the steps on the local screen and provide suggestions or actually take over the user's system to make the corrections. PC Tools from Central Point Software includes Commute, a program for both modem and network simultaneous access.

E-mail can be a very handy way to ask and answer noncritical problems. Writing the problem in the message logs it for both the user and the support staff. After a few months, the support staff can collect common problems and answers and provide an on-line help system or help manual.

"Ready for a Network?" Analysis Guide

There can be a lot of reasons for networking. There can also be a lot of reasons to postpone a network. Use this summary of reasons to make notes for or against a network in your location. Add your own reasons for and against a network in your location in the space provided.

> ✦ **Printers** Printers are commonly used on networks. Check their location to minimize user travel distance and the need for special paper insertion. The printer is likely to wear out quickly.

2

✦ **Hard disks** Hard disks are also commonly used on networks. This is not cost effective if it is the only reason to network. Be aware of the "all the eggs in one basket" advantage and disadvantage.

✦ **Modems** Establishing a communications server may make sense if many users rely on telecommunications a great deal.

✦ **Fax boards** Fax boards are a very handy way to communicate with other parts of the computerless world. They could save time if your fax machine is used frequently. It is difficult to fax anything not originating from the computer.

✦ **CD-ROMs** A CD-ROM provides great quantities of information. Check the CD-ROM license for LAN access.

✦ **File exchanging** One-way distribution of files can be very helpful. Limited access to write files is important.

✦ **Sequential file changes** Sequential file changes are useful within a work group. The process of making changes must be highly organized to be successful.

✦ **Simultaneous file changes** Simultaneous file changes require special LAN software and possible programming. They are the ultimate in LAN use, though.

✦ **LAN-based E-mail** E-mail is a delightful service waiting to be discovered on the LAN. There may be some reluctance to use it at first. Consistency of use is the key.

✦ **Scheduling** Scheduling is either a very powerful or very disruptive tool for the work group. Don't invest a lot of money without careful consideration.

✦ **Paperless office** The paperless office is becoming more possible with LANs and E-mail.

2

✦ **Group work** Effective use of the LAN can improve group communication and reduce the amount of paper flowing within the office.

✦ **Increased complexity** LANs increase the number of variables within the system.

✦ **More things to break** There is more equipment, more cables, and more connections to break in relation to the LAN.

✦ **Program conflicts** Making sure application programs work with the LAN can be difficult. LAN programs may cramp memory space.

✦ **Mission-critical tasks** Don't jump in with critical jobs before the LAN is stable.

✦ **Disaster preparation** The need to prepare for disasters is magnified on a LAN. The consequences of not planning can be even more disastrous.

✦ **Maintenance** There is more to take care of with a LAN. Using the file server for backup may or may not be a good idea, depending on users' backup habits.

✦ **Single-user software** Single-user software may not run on networks. Be careful with multiple users accessing single-user software on the server.

✦ **LAN software** LAN software is much safer to use on the LAN. It may make sense to purchase this even before establishing the LAN.

✦ **Support** The LAN provides new ways to provide support but also creates more problems that require help.

Summary

Any complicated decision requires a hard look at all the reasons for and against the results. This chapter has provided some of the specific advantages, disadvantages, and other reasons to consider a network. Use the analysis guide to evaluate your potential network. Keep in mind that these are not the only reasons to network. You may easily find more reasons. You may also find one or two overwhelming reasons not to network.

CHAPTER

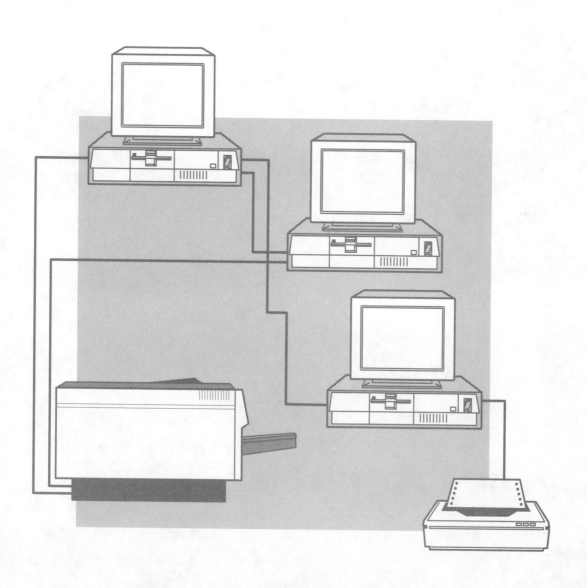

3 CAN YOU INSTALL A NETWORK?

Complete networks are now available in one package. These packages are a good place for beginning network administrators to start. This chapter provides suggestions to prepare you for installing a network. One approach is for you to prepare a list of people who may be able to help you install the network or answer questions you have. A checklist at the end of the chapter helps you evaluate your potential installation skills.

The previous chapters defined a network and provided reasons why you might want a network. You've also been exposed to several reasons why a network might not be a good idea in your situation. The next decision you need to make is whether or not you will install the network yourself.

Keep in mind that installation of the network is only the middle of the three steps covered in this book. The first part, design, is best done by someone familiar with the workflow—in other words, you. The last step relates to the maintenance of the network by the administrator. Again, the best person for this job will be you. This chapter relates to the actual installation of the hardware and software. Even if you have decided *not* to do this part yourself, reading this chapter will help you understand what you'll need from the individual or company installing the LAN. Chapter 9 provides more specific information about selecting and managing a network consultant.

The prospect of actually installing the network is not as daunting as it once was. Network software is more stable. Your current applications may have LAN versions, and several companies even provide a "network in a box," all software and hardware included. This chapter provides reasons why you might decide to install the network yourself. You'll see how to prepare for the operation by building a source for help. And finally, you can evaluate your skill level with a checklist.

Network Yourself

Even before you compare your skill level with those suggested for installing a network, you might want to consider several issues. These, like many other suggestions, are not the only approach you could use, but they present a useful perspective on network installation.

Go Slowly

The physician's oath to "at the very least, not leave a patient in any worse shape than when the treatment started" is a good starting point for a small network. The network should be another layer on top of the current computer systems. If the network replaces the current systems, you have placed a great deal more pressure on yourself and your users.

For example, if you decide to remove someone's hard drive and use it in the server, that user is unable to do anything without access to the network. That tactic won't endear you to the user either.

If you are accepting the responsibility for installing the network, you have to leave yourself the time and space to make a few mistakes. By taking a cautious approach to the installation, you can afford to learn how to do it right. Another example: don't assume that the first step after getting the network up and running is to immediately move that prized laser printer over to the server. If users were accustomed to handing the current owner of the laser printer a disk with the file to print, let that procedure continue for a few days. They've used that method for months; a few more days won't hurt. If you move the laser printer to the server and the network begins to crash every hour, no one will get laser-printed output.

Even as you design the network and consider installing it yourself, you want to carefully plan the steps to implement the network. You should take your time and proceed in minimal, reversible steps. Chapter 5 covers the planning process in more detail. Remember that even the smallest network can take weeks or months before it is completed. More likely, it will never really be completed; it will become just as functional as you can make it given the time and budget provided. Given more time and a larger budget, you can make it even more functional by adding features and resources.

Experience Pays

One major attraction for the do-it-yourself manager is the experience gained on the job. You know more intimately what goes into a project when you do the work yourself. With networks, this means you know where the cables are, which slots hold the network cards, and the choices made when installing the network software.

Every problem you solve helps you when a similar problem occurs. This is one of the main reasons, if not *the* main reason, to install the network yourself. You can begin building your repertoire of problem-solving strategies immediately. You'll find that you use them again and again.

Problems Encountered

The process of using a computer is the process of solving problems. From the most basic problem of learning that some keys do nothing by themselves (Alt and Ctrl) to that of a programmer trying to detect the Alt key when pressed, there are problems that everyone confronts and solves in one way or another. As the little problems are solved, the larger problems are also solved. These range from saving data entry time by starting a macro with Alt-M to writing a subroutine for scanning keyboard return codes.

The result of solving the largest problems is that it saves time or provides more information from the given data. The more successful the individual is at solving the little problems, the more that effect cascades into solving the largest of computer-related problems.

This suggests that a successful network installation requires the solving of problems—maybe a few, maybe a lot—and as the prospective designer/installer/supervisor, you must be quite proficient at it. You have to track them down, identify the cause, and discover the solution. You might even be the kind of person who enjoys solving problems. If you can't wait to climb into the network nest of problems and test your skills, so much the better.

Installation "Helpers"

People like to be helpful. The more they think they know about a subject, the more help they think they can be. This axiom certainly applies to installing a network. However, it is essential that one person control the installation. If you have several self-styled gurus, you may get help whether you want it or not. Be prepared to channel the helpful energy or deflect it elsewhere, or end up with an unusable network stew.

To minimize problems with the network, you'll need consistency. One advantage of installing a small network is that one person *can* do the majority of the work. You set all the card switches, you crimp the cable connections, and you install the software at each workstation. This provides that consistency. It also helps speed up the job because you learn a little bit more each time you repeat a task.

If someone tries to help, express that he or she is welcome but that you make the decisions. They can suggest, but you have the final vote. This is especially tough if your boss is trying to be helpful.

Here are a few tasks for your network helpers:

✦ Help toss cable running through the suspended ceiling.

✦ Sketch the actual location of the cables in the ceiling. (A building blueprint helps.)

✦ Unpack the manuals, removing cellophane wrapping.

✦ Make backup copies of the network software disks.

✦ Fill out the warranty cards for each network card and network software, including serial numbers.

✦ Write down the serial numbers of all the network cards and store with the original invoice.

✦ Stay one system ahead of you to remove the computer system covers.

✦ Go out and bring back lunch.

These are not trivial tasks. You'll need to do them if someone else doesn't. If you have a network consultant installing the network, these are tasks you can handle to save billable time.

Gathering Your Resources

Preparing to install a network is not the time to play "Lone Ranger." As you gain momentum on this project, you need to locate resources to help—specifically, people and companies. Research and develop this list as part of the preplanning process. The more resources you have, the less likely you'll be blindsided by problems and the more likely you'll be to solve problems once you discover them.

Each contact represents a person within your own company, another company, or just a friend down the street. The more information you have about these people, the more prepared you will be. Remember that you may not have to call any or all of them, but the names are there if you need them. A suggested form for your list is shown at the bottom of this page.

If the contact is a friend who is not going to charge you for his or her time, emphasize that help is a two-way channel—that although you are just in the startup phase, you will be glad to help later with any ideas or problems your friend wants to discuss with you.

When calling companies before you buy anything, emphasize that you are putting together a network and want to consider their product. Explain that you want to make a connection and will get back to them after you have narrowed your choices. Ask a few questions about their technical support:

✦ How long is the average wait to answer the call?

✦ For how many months after the purchase can you get support?

✦ Can one person remain your contact for calls?

✦ How much does support cost after the initial grace period?

Here is a suggested design for your contact list:

Last name: _____

First name: _____

Contact phone: _____

Fax: _____

E-mail address: _____

Hourly rate: _____

Hours available: _____

Company name: _____

LAN experience: _____

Cable/board experience: _____

Remote software: _____

3

Keep in mind that the larger your database of resources, the less you'll need to rely on one person or company. If you designate the people by areas of expertise, you won't have to keep calling on the same people throughout the process. For example, if you talk to someone about design, you should have someone else who can help with cabling questions. Don't abuse someone's offer to help. If you discover that you are relying on certain people a lot, at least offer to take them out to lunch. Or better yet, send a gift certificate for a nice meal for two. The last thing they may want to do is to talk to you over lunch.

Design Help

When looking for help with your network design, you need to find people who have designed networks and then worked with them for weeks or months. The professional network technicians can insert cards, throw cable, and install the network software, but they have not designed a network and then lived with it.

Find people who currently have networks and have an intimate knowledge of how well their network is running. If possible, examine their designs, even if the documentation is just something written down after the network was tossed together. If you have already decided on the network software, try to talk with people currently using the same program.

Try to find out how the network actually looks compared to their original design. Don't be too discouraged if it looks very different. You'll discover soon enough that changes are inevitable.

Hardware Help

Hardware help can come from several sources. The first could be the dealer who sold you the desktop computers. While they may not know much about networking overall, they may have heard about and helped people trying to install network cards in their systems.

A quick call to the company may help you rule out specific cards or networks they have found that don't work well in their systems, or they may have heard of specific systems that do work well. The company's systems may even be certified by specific networking companies. This assures you that the combination of computer system, network, and software will work together.

The manufacturer of the network cards is also likely to provide assistance. While they may or may not be willing to recommend a software package to be used with their cards, they may be willing to provide advice about specific types of cards they sell. Keep in mind that they may not have as much time to spend with you, a potential 3-card sale, as with the computer dealer on the other phone line who typically sells 50 cards a month.

Network technicians may not have the broadest range of experience but are likely to be helpful with specific cards or systems they have worked with. Make sure you negotiate the kinds of help they can provide and the cost. Their livelihood is based on your willingness to pay for their experience and knowledge.

Software Help

Software help may be harder to find on a casual basis. The company providing the LAN software is likely to help once you have purchased the software. They can help with the installation on the server and the workstations. If you are using a fairly standard network card, they may know of possible problems associated with that card. They are not as likely to be able to help with other software applications.

If you have purchased LAN versions of your software, you can reasonably expect help from that company. If you have neglected to register, you may have to explain that you are filling out the registration card even as you speak and will have the card in the mail before the day is out. Again, they are likely to have experience with more common networks and may have solutions readily available.

Keep in mind that the LAN, by its nature, combines software. The LAN represents another layer of software running on the workstation. No one can predict how every combination of software will work in your network. That's what you get to discover.

Cabling Help

When you develop your database of resources, keep in mind that you'll need help with this part of the installation. Running cable across

3

ceilings and down through walls is just plain hard physical labor. The farther away the workstations and the older the building, the more effort this can take. If you have suspended ceilings, you are also likely to have walls that extend just above the ceiling line but fall short of the roof. Tossing cable in this situation can be fairly easy and may take only an afternoon (see Chapter 6 for tips). If the building is older, the ceiling may be plaster or concrete. Running cable in this situation could take days, even with the right power equipment.

If you think you'll use a contractor to run the cable, look for someone with network wiring experience. Running network coax or twisted wire is not the same as running electrical wire. Don't let the contractor provide the cable unless you are sure he has exactly what you need. Licensed contractors also know local building and wiring codes. Throwing cables without knowing the local codes can cause problems should an inspector show up.

If you do decide to run the cable yourself, you may want to find one person with experience. He or she can provide the consulting while you stand on the ladder. You get to fight the dust-ball stampede in the suspended ceiling. A person with experience can also teach you how to make good connections on your cables.

You don't really want to go completely solo. Tossing cable really is a two-person job. Locate one or two people willing to wear jeans and climb a ladder for a day or two. The other person can stand on the second ladder to tell you how far off you are with each toss of the string.

"Nothing Works" Help

Above all, make sure you have a backup consultant available, at least by phone, while you work on the installation. Make sure this individual has worked with the hardware and software you are installing. Arrange the hourly rate before the first desperation call. Some consultants charge a minimum amount for each call, usually based on a fraction of their standard hourly rate. Others just charge by the minute. If you purchased everything from a dealer, ask how much help they are willing to provide over the phone. You may find that, within reason, you can rely on them with your first questions.

Paid professional help is the most important to have because there are so many variables in the process. As noted, each vendor may be able to give some help with their product, but when someone has to sort out all the pieces, direct experience with LANs is essential. You may also want to find out the consultant's on-site hourly rate. Even if you are totally stuck, you can have a lot of the basic work completed before you begin paying top dollar.

The phone support may cost $40 an hour or more with a 15-minute ($10) minimum. On-site support can easily be $75 an hour or more. As discussed in more detail in Chapter 9, those fees may be negotiable. Keep in mind that you have saved money because all the computer system covers have been removed, the cable has been pulled through the ceiling, and you are standing by ready to fetch a cold carbonated beverage any time the consultant looks thirsty.

Establishing Backup Support

Building the list of people and companies able to help is just the first step. The second step is using the best (read cheapest) communications channel. Included in the next sections are ways to obtain information about LANs.

Finding Help with E-mail

If you are familiar with on-line communications, you can find a great deal of information through your modem. Local bulletin board systems (BBSs) allow you to post a general message to see who reads and responds. A sample message might be

```
I am planning to install a network with 5 computers
attached. I think I need a dedicated server. All the
systems are within 100 feet of each other. I'm
interested in talking with anyone experienced in
setting up a small network. Interested in knowing what
software, board type, and cable. Please leave a message
or call direct at 302-555-6798.
```

If you subscribe to any of the commercial on-line services, you can find areas designated for networking and read the messages already posted. Those areas represent current discussions, some of which may mirror your questions or concerns. If, after reading the messages, you don't find a message to which you'd like to respond, you can post a message similar to the sample.

When you contact companies, you may want to ask if they have a BBS or a forum (special area) on a commercial service. If they run a BBS, the only cost to you is the long-distance call. The material on the BBS will be very specific to that company's product. Just reading messages can prove educational. Or, if they have a forum with an on-line service like CompuServe, you can also read messages about the product. Keep in mind that a vendor-run forum is not the same as a general forum. A general forum is run by people who do not have a vested interest in selling a specific product.

Even if you are not familiar with modems and using on-line services, ask around the office. There is a chance that someone knows how to tap into this local or commercial source of information with a modem. Let that individual be your intermediary. He or she can submit messages for you and print out the responses.

When you do locate people who can help through an on-line service, make a note of their names and their experiences in your resource database. With an on-line service, make sure you include their IDs in the record. If you are using a BBS, include the BBS phone number and the individual's exact name. Contacting these resources may not produce the quickest response, although some people do read and reply to their E-mail every day.

Using the modem to send E-mail has an additional advantage. You have to formulate the problem as carefully as possible. Just the process of writing down the problem may provide new insights. The response can be printed and studied as you return to the problem at hand.

One last note: Include as much information in the message as possible. This kind of message only irritates most readers who might have been willing to help:

```
Using NOVELL and can't get the workstations to print.
Any ideas?
```

Since you want to minimize the exchanges, provide as much information as possible in the first query:

```
Using NOVELL 2.2 on a nondedicated server. The
workstations can access the hard disk without a
problem. I've read the manual and don't understand how
to get the workstations to send printing to the laser
attached to the server.
```

This message tells the potential helper what the software is and what version you're using, as well as that some parts of the network are working. The message also shows that you have tried to use the manual but that the manual doesn't make any sense to you. That dilemma is universal. Your respondent is likely to suggest you try the CAPTURE command and may provide a few lines to explain print servers as well.

Phoning for Help

The popular phrase "reach out" is very applicable when you need help with your computer systems. The phone is an essential part of every installer's toolkit. One phone call can provide the answers to those problems that have stopped you dead in your tracks. If you have built your resource database, you know who you can call and may even have a backup person to call if the first person is unavailable.

As you build your resource list, think beyond your local calling area. Don't limit yourself to a local expert just because you don't want to make a long-distance call during the day. Even if you are calling across the country, the 25 cents a minute phone charge is still less than the $1 a minute fee you might pay to talk with a local consultant. Of course, your friend on the other side of the country can't come to the rescue if you need some on-site help.

We all know what is it like to hold the phone between your shoulder and ear for long periods of time. Your neck gets tired. Your ear gets hot and sweaty. With any luck, you won't have to make that kind of call when you install your network. On the other hand, you might want to consider purchasing a telephone headset. A small headset from your local electronics store can cost less than $50. The band slips over the head with one ear cushioned and the microphone extended in front of your mouth. Both hands are free to follow the suggestions offered on the other end of the call. You can comfortably talk, and type, for as long as you need with this arrangement.

As mentioned, don't overuse a person's willingness to provide free help. Keep your calls to a minimum. Make sure you have tried everything you can imagine before making the call. You might even jot down all the steps you have taken and recite those to explain what you have done. The helper on the other end can quickly see that you are calling because you are stuck. The process of discussing the problem can then be a brainstorming session for new things to try, not just repeating "I've done that already" for each suggestion.

If the caller begins to overwhelm you with suggestions, interrupt and explain that you can only "process" three at a time. Ask for a repeat of the first three. Then suggest that if those don't work, you would like to call back if that is okay. Make a phone appointment if that would be more convenient for the helper on the other end.

If you are paying a consultant for the call, being organized saves money. Prepare your list of attempts to solve the problem and list specific questions, if you know what they are. If the rate includes a minimum amount of time—for example, 15 minutes—have additional questions to ask to use the full 15 minutes you will pay for. At all times, be conscious that you control the call. Don't let the support person ask you to wait while he or she "looks it up." Insist that the person call you back when he or she has concrete suggestions for solving the problem.

When talking with a volunteer or a paid professional, keep in mind that while you control the call, you also need information, not counseling. Few things bother people more than hearing, "I just don't know what to do. I'm ready to toss the whole thing out the window." The quickest solution to their problem—you, the overwrought caller—is to encourage you to resolve the problem just the way you suggest. Toss it all out, and then you won't be calling them again. If you have to moan and groan, call a non-tech friend, get it all out, and then call your technical support.

Faxing for Help

When combined with follow-up phone calls, fax messages can save time when solving problems. They provide the immediacy of the phone call but also allow the support person time to consider the problem and form suggested solutions.

As noted in the "Finding Help with E-mail" section earlier in this chapter, state the problem as carefully as you can in the fax. List the attempted solutions. At the end of the fax message, include a time you plan to call. Depending on the company's fax delivery system, you may need to wait for a few hours. Or if you want to speed it up, send the fax, call the recipient, and let him or her know the fax is there. Then offer to call back at a convenient time. That person can then retrieve the fax with your questions and be prepared for your return call.

This method also works well when you are paying for the support. The recipient may (or may not!) charge for the time it takes to read the fax and research the answers. Depending on the complexity of the answers, the person might even fax back the response. If you plan to try this, leave space between questions; then he or she can write the responses next to the questions. While the original material will have been muddied twice by the fax process, the answers will have been sent only once. Since you have your original, you can read both the questions and the responses.

Using Remote Dial-in

A more sophisticated way to obtain help is with a connection directly from computer-to-computer. A number of programs allow two computers, each with a modem, to be connected via the phone lines. The second system, on the support end, shows exactly what is on the screen on the first system, on your end. Either one of you can type on your keyboard and affect your system. This is the next best thing to being there.

There are some limitations to this kind of arrangement:

+ You both must have a modem and phone connections.

+ You both must have a copy of the software.

+ You must load the software on your end to allow the incoming call. The support person must then call into your system with the same brand of software.

+ Running the software at your end may take up to 80K of memory, a precious commodity in some systems, considering the LAN software and the applications software running.

✦ Because you must run the receiving software before loading anything else, you can't expect remote help whenever you lock up the system.

✦ The keyboard response time can be rather slow, even with 2400-baud modems. Graphical environments can be glacial.

3

Even with those limitations, the experience can be invaluable. The best way to learn is to follow instructions given over a second phone line. (Remember the headset?) The support person can then watch you try the steps, providing corrections or suggestions from his or her end. You will have gained in two ways: you'll both know if the problem is resolved, and you'll have learned, step by step, how to solve the problem the next time it occurs.

Getting On-site Help

Your last-ditch backup plan is to have someone willing to come out to help you solve the network problems. This is not the same as having someone come out to install the network in the first place. You need to make the arrangements for this help before you get into trouble, but call only if you do get stuck.

Chapter 9 provides more information on how to deal with a consultant, but keep this in mind: If you do call someone to help, his or her first move may be to undo everything you have done so far. Network consultants normally start from scratch with installations rather than stepping into the middle. You can still learn a great deal from this help. Since you have already progressed to the problem point, you can compare your steps with those taken by the consultant. If you are lucky, you can see where you took the wrong path. And you will know you gave it your best shot.

"Can You Do It?" Checklist

Here is a checklist to help you decide whether or not to install the network yourself. Remember that this applies only to the actual hardware and network software installation. Even if you don't rate yourself very highly on this checklist, you will know about the installation process from this book.

1. Have you taken the cover off a computer and installed or replaced adapter cards such as video or hard drive cards?

2. Have you set dip switches and moved jumpers on cards?

3. Have you installed connectors on telephone and cable TV wires?

4. Have you routed telephone or coax cable through the existing ceilings and walls?

5. Do you understand what a TSR (terminate-and-stay resident) program is and (vaguely) how it works?

6. Have you installed large (multiple-disk) programs on hard drives?

7. Have you organized hard disks into logical subdirectories and arranged the program and data files?

8. Do you understand what the path is and how to change it?

3

9. Do you have the time and patience to devote to the installation above and beyond your current duties?

10. Are you prepared to read the manuals (and this book) carefully?

The more "Yes" answers on this checklist, the more likely you will be successful with self-installation. If you answered "No" to most of the questions from 1 through 8 but answered 9 and 10 as "Yes," you can still do it. Just make sure you purchase a network-in-a-box so you know all the components are compatible. Then, read the manuals carefully and take your time.

Summary

You'll do the planning. You'll do the maintenance. But you're not sure if you want to try the installation. This chapter has helped you decide. Even before you completed the checklist, you will have considered some approaches:

+ Plan to take your time. Even the simplest installation may take several days.

+ You are doing the installation because you want the experience of confronting and solving the problems.

+ You are going to maintain control of the installation by doing all the main jobs yourself.

You looked long and hard at the checklist. Even if you decided you wanted to have someone else do the main part of the job, you will prepare a list of people who can provide support before and after the installation. If you are going to do the installation yourself, you will definitely build a solid database of helpers' names.

Once the network is built, you can use a number of communication channels to get help:

✦ Use commercial and local on-line services to send E-mail messages and get replies.

✦ You can reach out and find help all across the country by phone.

✦ Faxes can be very helpful in clarifying the problem and getting a quick response.

✦ With preparation, you can use remote dial-in software and modems to get hands-on help.

✦ You can even have a fall-back position for the installation. Someone can come in and untangle your knots. Remember to keep them supplied with cold soft drinks, and don't get in the way as you help.

CHAPTER

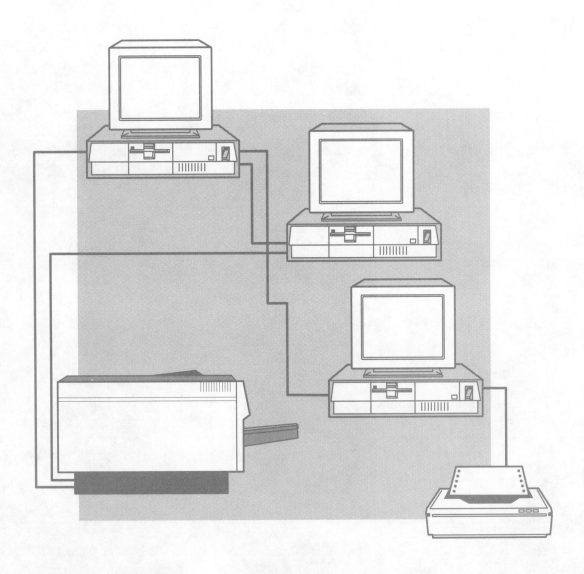

4

NETWORK COMPONENTS

Three components provide the connection to a network: the wire, the port, and the network software. Each part of this connection contains variables that must be resolved for the network to function properly. This chapter introduces you to the basic concepts you'll need as you begin to plan your network. The chapter worksheet helps you determine what your current equipment is and how it may be used to fit into the network.

The previous chapters covered the basic concepts of networking. This chapter examines the actual components necessary to create a LAN. The focus is on the practical information needed to install a LAN. Understanding these OSI specifications is necessary only when you are using different network protocols in large networks.

When making the connection between two or more computers, you must have three links in the chain. The first link is the software running on the workstation or server. The second link is the port in the computer, usually a network card. The final link is the actual medium, or cable, used to carry the signals from one computer to the next. Each of these links represents a variable you must consider when designing your network. Figure 4-1 shows these three links.

While Chapter 5 discusses the actual selection of these components, keep in mind that the software is the first concern when selecting a network. The network cards and cable type and arrangement are based on the selection of the LAN software. This chapter presents this information in reverse order because understanding the physical connections first helps when you start considering the software and the methods used by the software to make those connections.

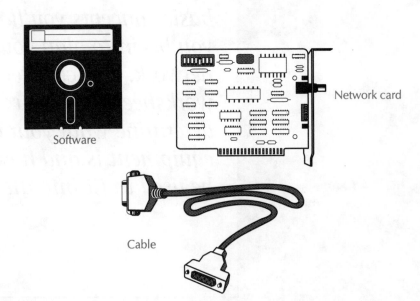

Software

Network card

Cable

The three pieces of the network connection
Figure 4-1.

Network Cards

The network card, located in your desktop computer, represents the middle and most potentially confusing part of the connection. Your selection of network software dictates the network protocol, which, in turn, dictates the speed at which your network can operate and the kind of cable you use. It also affects the cost per workstation since the higher-speed network cards are more expensive.

Different Computers, Different Cards

4

Like all cards that can be inserted in a desktop computer, network cards must match the system bus structure. The bus is physically represented on the bottom card edge that slides into the main system board. This bus is like a highway. More lanes in the highway allow more traffic. Even MS-DOS-compatible computers use different types of boards as well as different bus widths.

The cards designed for the original IBM XT have an edge with 30 gold-colored strips on each side. These cards are called *8-bit cards*. The main system board, also called the *motherboard,* has slots with an equal number of contacts on each side of the slot. Once the board is inserted in a slot, it becomes part of the computer. Figure 4-2 shows the bottom card edge and the slot in the motherboard.

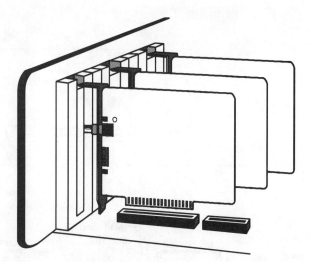

A card edge
and the
motherboard
slot
Figure 4-2.

Most desktop systems are based on the IBM AT computer design. This design is called the Industry Standard Architecture, or ISA. This design contains additional metal connectors on a second edge on the bottom of the card, with 18 contact points on each side, as shown here:

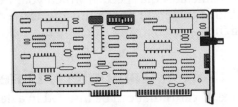

These cards are *16-bit cards*. These additional connections allow the signals from the motherboard to get to the network card more quickly (like extra lanes on the freeway).

The cards with just one set of contacts are 8-bit boards, while the cards with two edges are 16-bit boards. The 32-bit boards present in IBM PS/2 and other systems provide an even wider path. Network cards containing a 32-bit bus are more expensive and typically necessary only in high-speed servers.

You can use an 8-bit board with one edge in a system with two slots. You cannot use a card with two edges in a system with only one slot. Figure 4-3 illustrates these connections.

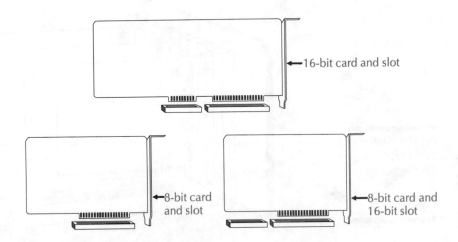

8- and 16-bit card compatibility
Figure 4-3.

Another card type is used in the IBM PS/2 system design, called the Micro Channel Architecture (MCA). These cards are totally different from the ISA systems and fit only in IBM PS/2-based systems and MCA-based PC compatibles. You may also hear about the EISA, which is the Extended Industry Standard Architecture. Systems based on this type of bus are able to use the ISA cards.

Also keep in mind that most laptop and notebook computers do not have additional slots for a network card. If a laptop does have a slot, it may have severe restrictions on the size, but it typically uses an ISA bus. The alternative for the laptop is an external parallel or printer port connector containing the network hardware.

Not only are the cards physically different, but the method used to send information through the cables (the network protocol) is also different, depending on the type of card. These protocols are incompatible with each other. With small networks, you cannot start building a network with one type of card and then add other types of cards. For example, if you start your network with Ethernet cards, you must stay with Ethernet. The brand of Ethernet card can be different, although you may introduce potential problems if you do change brands.

The Ethernet Protocol

For small networks, Ethernet has become the preferred network protocol. It provides a decent transmission speed when compared to the cost of the card and cabling. Depending on the version of the card you purchase, you can use more readily available types of cable.

Originally developed by Xerox Corporation in the 1970s, the Ethernet standard is capable of connecting up to 1024 workstations in a network. The transmission speed is rated at 10 megabits per second, although actual speeds are reported at closer to 2- to 3Mb (megabits) per second on standard Ethernet cards. The maximum length of cable between two workstations ranges from 500 to 1500 feet.

NOTE: Network traffic is measured by transmission of the basic elements (bits) from one station to another. A megabit represents approximately 1 million bits. The actual transmission speed in a specific network depends on a number of factors. Megabits (Mb) provide a common standard measurement.

The Ethernet standard gaining popularity is the 10Base-T, in part because it uses the more easily installed twisted-pair cable. On the less positive side, this Ethernet and twisted-pair cable combination requires a concentrator (central) box in the network. This concentrator could cost more than $400. On a very small network with just two or three workstations, this expenditure increases the average workstation cost significantly. On a larger network of seven to ten stations, the cost is less per station. You may find, though, that the ease of using twisted-pair cable may outweigh the extra cost of the concentrator.

While prices on computer products can vary a great deal, prices for Ethernet boards can range from $150 for an 8-bit coax to $250 for a 16-bit 10Base-T board. These prices may be even lower when you purchase the boards with the network software.

When purchasing Ethernet boards, you must check to see whether the board is standard or proprietary. For example, the LANtastic peer-to-peer network software requires boards sold by Artisoft. This company's approach is to tie their software into their boards. The software provides for up to 300 users, but you are required to purchase the company's network card for each workstation. (You will find more details on the LANtastic system in Chapters 6 and 7.)

The ARCnet Protocol

ARCnet was the standard network adapter card for years. Originally developed by Datapoint Corporation, ARCnet cards are contained in many LANs running today. With the price reductions in and improved speed of Ethernet cards, ARCnet cards are not usually recommended for networks today. In fact, you'll need to check carefully to make sure your network software has ARCnet drivers. For example, NOVELL's NetWare Lite is a very easy system to install, but the software does not include drivers for ARCnet cards.

The only advantage to ARCnet now is rock-bottom prices. The prices have dropped from over $300 in the mid-1980s to under $100 today, if you can find them. The rated transmission speed of only 2.5Mb per second is sluggish performance when compared to Ethernet cards, considering the actual transmission is even slower. This limited transmission speed is very noticeable on the 386 systems but not as critical on slower XT and AT systems.

ARCnet cards make sense if you meet these conditions:

✦ You need a very small network for three to five users.

✦ There will be no need to add more stations.

✦ The network is mostly needed for printer sharing.

✦ You have an extremely tight budget.

Above all, if your company begins to grow, write off the ARCnet cards and replace them with Ethernet. Don't think you are saving money in the long run by continuing to buy inexpensive ARCnet cards. Also realize that the cable is different for Ethernet. To make the switch, you need to pull the old ARCnet cable and replace it with Ethernet cable.

Other Card Types

There are a number of other types of network cards available. These include Token-Ring and Fiber Distributed Data Interface (FDDI). Some companies also produce proprietary network card systems. All these cards are typically used in much larger networks.

Another type of card eliminates the need to run cable from system to system. Dubbed "wireless LANs," this method of connecting desktop systems is still in its infancy. The signal used with these systems is radio or infrared. None of these systems use the same data transmission method, and they connect to the workstations in different ways. The distance between stations is also limited and may be affected by intervening objects. Some require "line-of-sight" for transmission.

Wireless networks make sense if workstations are frequently moved around the office or if you are unable to run cable between systems. You'll need a healthy budget as well. A five-station LAN is likely to cost over $5000 for the hardware alone.

Connections and Cable Types

The signal carried from system to system is very sensitive and requires a very specific type of cable. Each cable, in turn, requires a specific connector. The choices for cable are affected by the network card (protocol), cable layout, possible electromagnetic interference, and, of course, your budget.

Coaxial Cable and BNC Connections

Coaxial cable, abbreviated "coax," looks like the cable used to bring the cable TV signal to your television. One strand (a solid-core wire) runs down the middle of the cable. Around that strand is insulation. Covering that insulation are braided wire and possibly metal foil, which shields against electromagnetic interference. A final layer of insulation covers the braided wire. Figure 4-4 shows coax as well as twisted-pair and fiber optic cables.

Just because the TV cable is coax does not mean it will work with networks. Network coaxial cable has very specific requirements such as the gauge, the impedance, and attenuation. Fortunately, these characteristics are grouped into cables designated for networks. The manual with your network cards will explain the exact type of cable required for the board. For example, the required coaxial cable might be designated RG58A/U or RG58C/U. These codes are likely to be printed on the cable and on the cable spool.

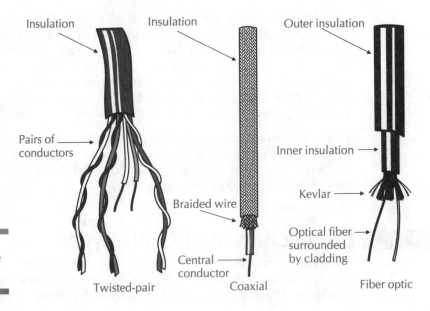

Three main types of cable
Figure 4-4.

4

Coaxial cable for Ethernet networks is further divided into Thick Ethernet, or just Thicknet, and Thin Ethernet, or Thinnet. This cable is specifically designated as RG-8. It is rated to carry a signal 500 meters (1500 feet). The cables may have a yellow PVC (plastic) covering or an orange plenum (fire-resistant) covering. Thicknet is frequently used to combine signals into a "backbone" on networks encompassing several floors of workstations.

Thinnet is the coax cable you are most likely to use with your Ethernet cards. This cable is fairly flexible and much easier to work with than Thicknet. Transmission is limited to 180 meters (500 feet) between stations. This cable uses BNC connectors and sleeves of .2-inch diameter. The cable designation is RG-58. As always, check in your Ethernet card manual for additional specifications.

Thinnet coaxial cable uses BNC connectors, as shown here:

These connectors use a twist-to-lock sleeve that attaches to the T-connector on the back of the network card or other devices on the network. You can attach the connector to the cable only after carefully stripping the insulation from each layer. Once the cable is inserted, you must crimp the sleeve a specified pressure, using a special tool. While Chapter 6 explains this in greater detail, note that the process of attaching the BNC connectors requires precise work. Many network problems can be traced to poor cable connections.

TIP: Plan to purchase proper cable tools as part of the entire cable installation. While the tool set may cost up to $100, it is well worth the expense. The cable supply company can also be a source for the proper tools.

Coaxial cable is not easy to install. It cannot be pulled into a sharp 90-degree angle and requires careful attachment to the BNC connectors.

Depending on the cable type, it can cost from \$.14 to \$.42 per foot. Unless you plan to install wall sockets, you'll need to attach only BNC plugs to the cable.

Twisted-pair Cable and RJ-45 Connectors

Twisted-pair wire cables are familiar to you if you have worked with phone cable. Each of the pair of wires contained in the cable is twisted around the other. The typical twisted-pair cable rated for network use contains three or four pairs of wires. This arrangement helps shield against electromagnetic interference.

Because this wire is similar to phone wire, some network installations attempt to use the phone wiring already installed in the building for the network connections. Problems are guaranteed when these voice-grade lines are used in a data-grade application.

Phone wires are rated as level 1 for transmission of voice, while the minimal recommended level for networks is level 3. At level 3, the cable must be able to transmit at 10Mb, the rate for Ethernet used today. Transmissions at 16Mb and 20Mb are also included in levels 4 and 5, respectively.

NOTE: Carefully consider the expected growth of the network against the current cost of the cable. Some consultants recommend using the level 5 cable, which costs 20 times as much as level 3 cable, anticipating that much increase in transmission speed in the near future. Note that you can use old cable to pull new cable if your data transmission needs should increase later.

The twisted-pair cable uses small plastic connectors designated as RJ-45. These are similar to the phone connectors except that instead of the four wires found in the home system, the network RJ-45 contains eight contacts. Attaching these connectors to twisted-pair cable requires a special tool to force the contacts in the plastic into the inserted wires. Those contacts then rest against contacts in the socket once the RJ-45, shown here, is snapped into place:

Twisted-pair cable is easier to install than coaxial; you can pull it around corners more easily. Twisted-pair cable is more susceptible to interference and should not be used in environments containing large electrical or electronic devices. Each of the eight wires must be exactly lined up in the RJ-45 connectors before it is crimped. As with coax and BNC connectors, making a good connection can be a major problem. Depending on the cable type, it can cost from $.05 to $.11 per foot. (See Chapter 6 for an installation tip when using a twisted-pair cable network.)

CAUTION: As with all cables, refer to the network card documentation or contact the network card company for the exact specifications on the cable you need to run the network. Do not accept advice to use the voice-grade (level 1) twisted-pair cable already installed in the building.

Fiber Optic Cable

The Fiber Distributed Data Interface (FDDI) specifies data transmission speeds of up to 100Mb. FDDI provides many advantages in addition to the high data transmission speed. It supports up to 1000 stations and can carry the signal up to and beyond 50 miles. Fiber optic cable is also highly secure from outside interference. On the other hand, it is by far the most expensive of these cabling methods, and a small network is unlikely to need these features.

Topology

The way the stations are physically connected is called the network *topology*. The three main LAN topologies are bus, ring, and star. The selection of the network card types and software dictates the actual

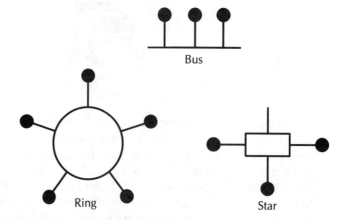

The three topologies
Figure 4-5.

arrangement of cables. The topology is a much more critical issue for larger networks. Figure 4-5 shows these topologies.

The *bus topology* is the most common and used for most Ethernet installations. The cable is threaded from station to station, attaching to each computer, and then continuing to the next station. The bus topology is the easiest topology to install and maintain since the connections represent a line from the beginning to the ending station. Keep in mind that the server(s) can be located anywhere in the thread and that a break in the cable can bring down the whole network.

The *ring topology* forms a continuous, closed path. The actual signal is regenerated by each station and results in longer transmission distances and higher data transmission rates. This topology also lends itself to fiber optic cabling.

The *star topology* looks more like a tree. Signals are sent from level to level via hubs. The message works its way to the top and is then rebroadcast down to all stations. Large LANs are able to use the star topology more effectively when connections cross departments and move from floor to floor.

Slotless Systems

You can construct a minimal, two-to-four-station LAN without a network card of any type. These slotless systems make their

4

connections by using the serial and parallel ports on the desktop systems. There is no card to insert in the computer.

The slotless LAN connects these systems very inexpensively. The main reason to connect systems in a slotless LAN is to share printers and hard disk space. This type of network is really a limited "peer-to-peer" (see the section "Peer-to-Peer Software" later in this chapter). Some vendors provide additional services in their LAN package. A typical two-station slotless LAN could contain a laptop and desktop system. Cable requirements are also minimal. If not supplied with the network, you can construct the cables with 9-wire serial cable, ribbon cable, or standard flat phone cable.

Serial Connections

The cable required to connect systems in a slotless LAN differs from standard serial cable used to connect a modem or other serial device. Because computers have a 25- or 9-contact plug (you can see the contact), the cable must have a receptacle on both ends. It must also be a null modem cable. This kind of cable has specific wires crossed to allow the serial ports to exchange data.

In lieu of purchasing a special cable, you can use a standard plug-and-receptacle serial cable, a gender changer, and a null modem adapter to arrive at the same configuration. However, this combination of connectors is likely to be more expensive than just finding a receptacle-to-receptacle null modem cable. Figure 4-6 shows a serial plug, receptacle, and null modem adapter.

Serial cables are either ribbon (flat) or shielded. The ribbon cable is much easier to work with if the slotless LAN software includes a wiring diagram. With a little patience and supplies from a local electronics

A serial plug, receptacle, and null modem adapter
Figure 4-6.

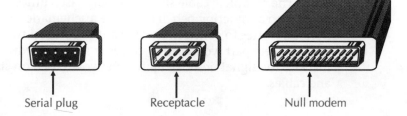

Serial plug   Receptacle   Null modem

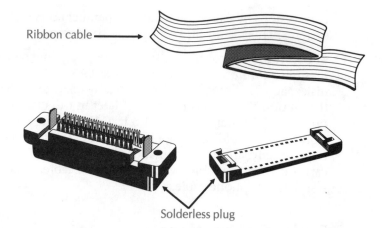

Ribbon cable

Solderless plug

A ribbon cable
and solderless
plug
Figure 4-7.

store, you can make your own receptacle-to-receptacle null modem
cable. Figure 4-7 shows ribbon cable and the solderless plug.

Some vendors provide all the cable necessary in their slotless LAN kits.
These kits may include a special adapter for the serial or parallel port
that contains the RJ-11 (phone clip) receptacle. To connect the systems,
the plug is inserted into the port and then the phone line is clipped
into the back of the plug. Check with the vendor concerning the cable
lengths and range. You still may have to construct some cables to meet
your needs.

The ribbon cables are limited to very short distances, less than six feet.
If the two connected systems are very close together, these unshielded
ribbon cables may work. You press the clamps together on the
solderless plug to make contact through the ribbon cable. The null
modem connector then makes the necessary crossovers for the cable to
work.

With longer distances, up to 60 feet, you need the round, shielded
cable. The complete cable should be purchased unless you are very
adept with a soldering pencil and have a schematic showing the
necessary wires to connect. If you want to connect two systems more
than 60 feet apart, you need to consider special hardware adapters that
increase the signal or move up to a network based on standard cards
and cables.

Parallel Connections

The parallel port also represents a way to connect two systems in a slotless LAN. The system end of the parallel port utilizes the same 25-contact plugs used in serial cabling. The difference is that the parallel port uses the receptacle end on the back of the computer. The parallel-to-parallel connection between two systems requires a special plug-to-plug cable designed to be used with a slotless LAN. Check with the vendor for this special cable.

CAUTION: Because the only difference between the parallel and serial ports on some systems is the gender, it is possible to attach one system's serial port to another system's parallel port. Newer systems also contain the 9-pin plugs for one or both of the serial ports. If you make this mistake, you may damage one or both computer systems.

Network Software

Even though this section on network software follows the discussion on cards and cables, the software is the first part of the network you need to make a decision about. Before you could consider the software, you needed to know about network cards, cables, and topology. Now you are ready to learn about the three main categories of network software: slotless, peer-to-peer, and server-based.

Slotless Software

The most basic slotless network provides the minimal features of a network: disk and printer sharing. Once connected, each system's drives and printer ports are available to the other systems. A few vendors' products also include E-mail and some security. Check this type of LAN carefully to see what features are supported.

Installation may consist of installing several device drivers in CONFIG.SYS and running the program. For example, THE $25 NETWORK includes an installation program. Once the serial cable is connected, the program asks a few questions and then copies the basic files to the disk. Once the systems are rebooted, they should be able to share drives and printers. The package includes a program to check for the available serial ports and to test the cable connection. More experienced users can just add the necessary lines to the CONFIG.SYS and AUTOEXEC.BAT files manually.

A slotless network provides a very inexpensive and easy way to connect computers. High performance is not to be expected when the signals travel through the serial port. On the other hand, copying small files and sending print jobs between systems is not excessively slow. You must also keep in mind that this kind of network has no hope of providing multiple access to databases or operating under a heavy workload. Some vendors provide up to eight connections, but this type of network is better used with four or fewer stations.

A slotless network can be very inexpensive. THE $25 NETWORK includes the cost as part of the title. Even products designed to handle four stations can cost as little as $400. Keep in mind that each system requires a serial port. If the computer systems have only one serial port and that is used for a mouse, you must install an I/O card with another serial port or replace the single-port serial card with a dual-port card. These cards cost under $50.

Peer-to-Peer Software

A peer-based network can use the resources of all the systems attached to the network. These resources include hard drive space and printers. Potentially, every printer and every hard drive on the network could be used by anyone else on the network. This would be like anyone in the work group coming in and sitting down at your desk to do their work. Practical considerations usually prevent that kind of access.

Installation of peer-to-peer networks is designed for ease of use. Insert a disk in a drive, type the letter of that drive, and then type **Install**. The program prompts for all the necessary data about the server or workstation. If the system is a workstation only, the file space requirements are minimal. If the workstation will also function on the network as a server, more files will be copied to the hard disk. In many cases, the network software is contained on one disk and takes a relatively small amount of local disk space. The entire installation may take as little as 30 minutes, provided you have already prepared your LAN design.

Peer-to-peer LAN software is usually purchased per workstation. For example, NetWare Lite has a suggested retail price of $100 per workstation. You purchase one manual and software disk for each individual station on the network. The software for that workstation is installed from that individual disk. Notice that this does not include the cost of the network card.

LANtastic uses another approach. Two Ethernet cards are included in the LAN starter kit along with the network software. While the software can be installed on up to 300 systems, you have to purchase additional Ethernet cards designed for LANtastic at $200 each. Once the starter kit is purchased at $699 list, each station to be connected to the network costs $200, plus cable.

4

Like most software, performance and ease of use must be balanced. The more powerful a program is, the more difficult it is to use. Because a peer-to-peer system is designed to be easy to use, performance is likely to be adequate but not spectacular. The actual performance of a specific software package depends on the number of users, the network cards, and the demands being made on the software. Peer-to-peer, by its design, is sharing processor power with other applications on each system that is set up as a server. The actual response time will depend on the additional tasks being performed by those servers.

Server-based Software

A server-based LAN uses one machine as the hub of the network. While some server duties may be assigned to other workstations, one system serves as the focal point for the network files. In a dedicated server setup, this system may just serve the network and not be available for anything else. This dedicated system cannot be used as a workstation. Some server-based networks, such as NOVELL NetWare 2.2, allow the server to also function as a workstation, making it a nondedicated server. In both cases, dedicated and nondedicated, one system is typically the center of the small LAN.

Installation of a server-based network is likely to be more complicated than peer-to-peer networks. For example, NetWare 2.2 takes over the hard disk on a server. To do this, it compiles the network operating system based on the network cards and desktop computer. The process requires over eight disks and may take several hours. If the server is also to function as a workstation, additional steps are required. Each workstation must have a copy of the network program created for that machine as well. This does not take as much time as installing the server software.

Server-based LANs are sold in increments. For example, NetWare 2.2 starts with a minimum of five users and jumps to ten. The list price for the five-user version is $895, and the list for the ten-user version is $1995. If you want six users on the network, you still must purchase the ten-user version. The number of users is embedded in the copy of the software. You can increase the number of users with a special upgrade purchase.

Server-based LANs are fine-tuned for the best performance. Considering the time and expense, this is as expected. A network with ten stations and a lot of network traffic may need the higher performance of this more complicated network program.

Planning Worksheet

Even before you design the entire network—and even before you have selected your network software—you can begin to list the parameters you have to work with. These include the machines, the cable access, and the available printers. Use these steps to outline the physical requirements of your LAN:

1. List each system to be attached to the LAN. Check to make sure an extra slot is available with either the 8-bit or 16-bit bus or whether the machine uses the MCA bus. Note that an 8-bit card may be in a 16-bit slot and can be moved to free up the 16-bit slot.

2. Obtain or sketch the office layout. Mark the location of each station to be attached to the LAN. Include any printers to be shared across the LAN.

3. To the office sketch, add the cable runs from station to station. If you think you might use a star topology, estimate the locations for the star concentrator/hub(s).

4. Look for the most reasonable location for the main server. While the server can be anywhere when using the bus topology, if it also has printers attached, users need access to the printers.

5. Estimate the length of each cable run from the sketch. Keep in mind that if you are installing through the ceiling, you need to add the distance up the wall for each station. Leave at least an extra five feet of cable. Leave even more if you think the station could be relocated within the room.

6. Try to visit at least one other location using the same or a similar layout for cabling a LAN. Ask how long their cable installation took and who did it. At the worst, you'll see an example of how not to run the cable.

7. Locate a resource for at least two stepladders that reach to the ceiling. The maintenance staff may loan you these ladders.

8. Check to make sure you will not be violating any work site rules if you install the cable yourself. This may be considered an electrician's duties.

9. Also check local building codes. These codes dictate the location of wires. For example, you need to use fire-resistant cable when running over ceiling panels. This may affect the entire decision process. You may find that you can't use certain cable because of the building codes. You may have to rethink your software and network card choices so you can use allowable cable.

Summary

This chapter covered the three components necessary to connect desktop computers: the port (usually the network card), the cable, and the software.

✦ To make the network connection, you need a way to get the signal to the network cable. This could be a serial or parallel port but will more likely be a network card.

✦ The most popular cards are now Ethernet because of the price/performance ratio. ARCnet cards are very inexpensive but provide slower transmission speed. Using the serial or parallel ports is the cheapest method but is significantly slower than using a network card.

✦ The cable connecting these systems is based on the card type, the most common being twisted-pair and coaxial. These cable types are very specific. You cannot use the wrong cable and expect the network to function.

✦ Cable connections are very delicate. Expect to spend trial-and-error time if you decide to attach the connectors to the cable yourself. If you have problems, suspect your cable connections first.

✦ Network software can spread the network load out to each station in peer-to-peer systems or concentrate the load on a server. Peer-to-peer systems tend to cost less, while server-based systems provide better performance. Slotless systems are typically used for just two computers, when a high transmission speed is not critical.

C H A P T E R

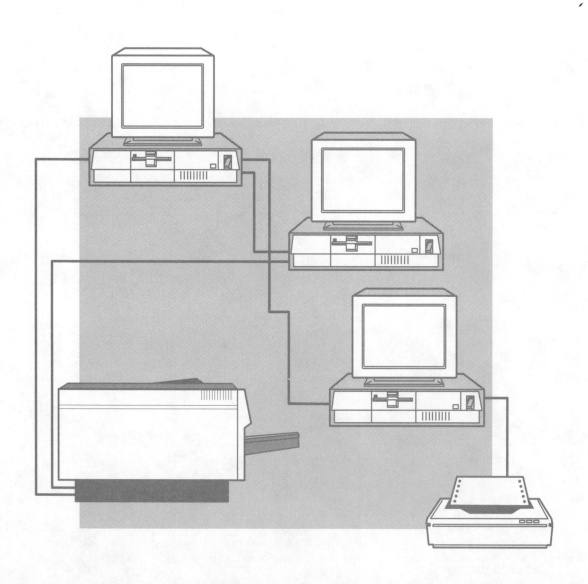

5

PLANNING THE NETWORK

By now, you have an idea of what you want to accomplish with a small network. At this point, you need to gather your notes and worksheets together to develop your network plan. You need this plan even if you have decided to let someone else install the network. You can prepare a plan using the worksheets and checklists you completed at the end of each of the previous chapters.

Chapter 1 provided a definition of a LAN. Chapter 2 explored the advantages and disadvantages of installing a LAN. Chapter 3 helped you decide whether or not you will install the network yourself. Chapter 4 laid out all the parts required to create a LAN. If you have been completing the checklists and worksheets at the end of each chapter, you have the start of your network plan. Even if you decide not to do the installation yourself, you still need to prepare a strategy. This chapter takes the information you've gathered so far, presents additional information, and provides an outline for your network plan. But first, you'll meet Bob and Tom, who'll show you how *not* to install a network.

How Not to Install a Network

Suspend, just for a few pages, your concerns about the network you are planning, and watch instead a team of two install their first LAN. Make notes on a separate sheet of paper when you notice potential problems. You'll have a chance to compare your notes against a summary of the problems later in the chapter. As you cover material later in this chapter and in Chapters 6 and 7, you'll find solutions to these and other network problems.

The team is installing a network consisting of six workstations, each in a separate office down one side of a hall. The main purpose of the network is to use the laser printer in the boss's office and to send phone

messages to everyone in the work group. The network software has been selected because it provides printer sharing and has an E-mail feature built-in.

The chronicle starts on a bright Monday morning with the team, Bob and Tom, opening the box containing the network software and hardware. Bob begins digging the packages out, scattering plastic foam peanuts all over the floor. One package contains a starter kit with two network cards, 25 feet of cable, one disk containing the network software, and various manuals. The additional four boxes contain network cards.

Bob is the office computer enthusiast. He installs all the software for everyone. He has experience in installing hard drives and has upgraded several systems in the office to VGA display cards and screens. When anyone needs help with a computer, Bob gets a call. He has never installed a LAN and never used one. He did read an article about LANs, though.

Tom is the enthusiastic novice computer user. He has installed some software but has never looked inside a computer. He wouldn't know a dip switch if he saw one and has only a vague notion of subdirectories.

Bob keeps his set of tools in his desk drawer. The kit contains several flat and Phillips screwdrivers, wire cutters, a small hand mirror, and a small surgical clamp called a hemostat. Today he brought his power screwdriver from home.

Jumping in too Quickly

Bob immediately turns off his system, removes the cover, and sticks in the network card. He slips the cover back on and restarts the system. He inserts the disk from the starter kit, switches to drive A, and types **Setup.** That doesn't work, so Bob types **Install.** That starts the network installation program. In every case, he chooses the manufacturer's default settings and the program copies the files to his hard disk. Once finished, he reboots the system. Since the installation program has modified the AUTOEXEC.BAT file, the network software starts—or tries to start. The message says, "No server found."

Since the software loaded, the card must be working. Bob decides the only problem is a missing server. Since the printer they want to share is in their boss Nancy's office, that system should be the server. The team just has to connect all the cables and then there will be a server for Bob's system to "find."

The starter kit has only one section of cable. Bob and Tom study that cable. It is labeled RG 58A/U. Since each office is 10 feet wide, and there are six offices down one side of the hall, they must need 60 feet of cable—make that 70, just in case. Bob sends Tom out to find the RG 58A/U cable. He gives Tom a connector from the back of the card to find the right kind of ends for the cable.

Upsetting the Users

While Tom visits several local electronic supply stores looking for the cable, Bob goes from office to office telling everyone to turn off their desktop systems within the next ten minutes. He assures them that the systems should available by 11:00, "no problem." He ignores the dirty looks from several users. That, after all, is the price of progress.

Bob turns off the computers. Using his power screwdriver, Bob removes the cover, inserts the network card, and puts the cover back on each system. "No," he tells everyone, "you can't use it yet. We have to connect the cables and install the software." Bob returns to his desk and studies the morning paper. Tom finally returns with the cable. "Great, now we're almost finished."

They start in Tom's office, the farthest down the hall. Bob coils the cable on the floor. He stands on a desk and is just able to push the ceiling tile up. Tom waits on the other side of the wall for the cable to snake over. He is wedged between a bookcase and the credenza. Once he has the cable, he pulls 60 feet of cable over the wall. Bob comes over to the second office (his) with his wire clippers. He stretches the cable to the back of the system and makes a quick cut. With a pocket knife and pliers, they strip the insulation off the cable, jam the connector on, and pinch the sleeve on the connector with pliers. Once connected, the cable stretches from the system, up the wall, over the dividing wall, and down to the next system.

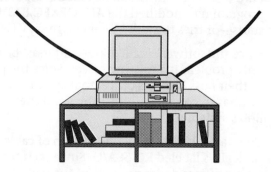

Network Planning

The network warriors proceed from office to office, stringing the cable. Bob knocks over a plant. Tom manages to spill someone's coffee. They run out of cable on the fourth office. Tom is sent out for more cable and for lunch.

As Tom admires Bob's adept use of chopsticks on Kung Pao Chicken, they discuss the network. They decide that the easiest way to set up the network is to allow everyone to share the hard disk in the server as drive F on their local system. Then, if anyone needs extra storage space, he or she can use F to save files. Since everyone wants to use the laser printer in Nancy's office, that will be LPT2 on everyone's system. To use the electronic mail feature, they'll create a batch file called ELECTRON.BAT to access the LAN E-mail system.

They finish throwing and connecting the cable by mid-afternoon. Each office now has a black "V" on the back wall, created by the cable running from each adjacent office. Their office cohorts stopped believing "real soon now" right after lunch. Once again, Bob and Tom return to each office to install the network software. They notice a distinct chill in each office they visit. They reboot each machine to start the network. Once again, the software stops with an error message: "No server found."

LAN Supervisor by Chance

The pair arrives in Nancy's office and is relieved to find the boss gone for the afternoon. They install the software and make sure this system is the server. Tom installs the users' names, including Nancy, and gives them all the same password, "chopstick." Bob and Tom think this is a great trick. Since they'll tell everyone to keep their password secret, no one will know they all have the same password.

They discuss who should be the supervisor on the LAN and toss a coin to settle the issue. The winner is Nancy. The loser is Nancy's secretary. Bob dutifully assigns supervisor status to Nancy's account.

Not Enough User Training

Tom runs down the hall to check each system. The error message is gone on most of the systems. The last two offices, Bob's and Tom's, still have the error. Bob goes into the third office from the end and wiggles the cable. Tom yells out that the systems are running now. "All fixed."

Bob and Tom fan out to provide instructions to the three users currently in their offices. Each shows the user how to log on to the network using his or her name and secret password. Bob explains that to use the laser printer in Nancy's office, the user must tell his or her software to use LPT2 instead of LPT1. Tom carefully explains that all printing now goes to Nancy's office and solemnly cautions against printing resumes on the network. To one user, Bob mentions that drive F is now available to save files. Both Bob and Tom provide helpful yellow stickers with the word "electron" to remind users how to start the E-mail program.

By the time Bob and Tom finish the network training, the last person is 15 minutes late leaving the office. Bob and Tom leave to celebrate the successful installation of their first network.

Major Problems

The next day, Bob arrives at work a little late, suffering from the party the night before. Bob senses trouble when he sees the note from Nancy

in the middle of his desk. He considers inviting Tom along to the "instant meeting" but decides against it. When he arrives at Nancy's office, he isn't prepared for the storm.

Nancy explains, in a voice just short of a roar, that there seem to be a few problems with the network installation. She hands Bob a list, explaining that this was all she could do this morning since she couldn't use her system. This is Nancy's list:

+ I can't use my system. No one gave me the password.

+ Jane keeps coming into my office to get printouts.

+ George and Martha keep typing "electron" as their password and it won't work. They can't use their systems either.

+ The cables running down the walls are hideous.

+ Bob or Tom ruined a report with spilled coffee.

+ The overturned plant will probably die.

+ No one was able to work on his or her computer all day yesterday.

+ Where is this electronic mail Bob promised?

Nancy knows just the half of it. In addition to her issues, there are a few more problems and potential problems that she has not encountered. Here are some of the solutions:

✦ Planning the network is the first step.

✦ Start a project on Saturday or after office hours. Immediately locate and keep the invoice/packing list. Check the actual items against the items showing as shipped.

✦ Know how a functioning LAN is supposed to operate before you install one.

✦ Prepare a list of secondary tasks for helpers.

✦ Use the hand mirror to look at the back of each system. The hemostat helps recover screws dropped into tight places. The power screwdriver can be very handy but too much force can easily strip threads on the screws.

✦ Turn off the power and disconnect the power cord. Ground yourself before handling cards. Read the manuals. Make a backup copy of AUTOEXEC.BAT or CONFIG.SYS files. Create a boot disk to use if the installation locks up the system.

✦ Check the connector size against the proper size cable. Planning includes estimating cable length.

✦ Call ahead to check for the availability of materials, including wiring and connector supplies. Don't do the work while others are waiting to use their systems.

✦ Check to make sure the cards are being inserted in the appropriate 8- or 16-bit slots. Replace the cover after the cards have been tested. Fill out the warranty cards.

✦ Always use a ladder.

✦ Pull the short end of the cable across the wall.

✦ Consider all the possible paths.

✦ Plan ahead to avoid shortages.

✦ Leave slack cable. Always use the special clamping tools for cable connections.

5

- ✦ Use batch file names that make sense.

- ✦ Install the server first.

- ✦ Allow all users to create their own passwords.

- ✦ Pick the network supervisor carefully.

- ✦ Solve problems permanently, don't just wiggle wires.

- ✦ Plan and provide consistent user training. Training on different parts of the network may be spread out over several sessions but schedule these sessions ahead of the installation.

- ✦ Test, test, test the network. Prepare printed information explaining the network.

The network Bob and Tom built may work. They may even be able to show users how to wiggle cable to correct disconnections. Nancy may learn to encrypt her sensitive files to avoid snooping. But this is a network in physical connections only. It is destined to have physical and user problems for as long as Bob keeps his job.

Now that you've seen how *not* to install a network, you can discover the finer points of proper network planning and installation.

Start with a General Plan

Even the smallest of networks requires a plan. The planning covers the hardware and software installation, resource organization, and user training. The more completely you think about the network, the better you'll be able to anticipate some of the problems. But it is only fair to mention that your final network installation is likely to differ from your original plan. Make notes on the original plan as you make changes to the design.

Even before you begin to lay out the resource sharing on the network, you need to decide how dependent on the server the users will be. You can design the network so that users must use the server constantly or just for printer sharing. The following sections show five ways to design the file-sharing system. You may want to place a check mark next to the advantages and disadvantages listed after each design that fits your situation.

NOTE: When discussing the use of files on the server, the server is called the *"file server."* When the server has printers attached, it is called a *"print server."* In most small networks, the server is usually both a file server and a print server. In this book, the term "server" applies to all configurations.

Server Programs, Server Data Files

You can use one or more systems as file servers in a network. Typically, on a small network, just one system contains the files users need. One way to set up the network is to have all program and data files on the server's hard disk. For example, any time users want to run a program, they are actually reading the file from the file server and running the program on their system. The data files they use and save are also on that same server's disk. The user's local disks are not used except to boot the system and to log onto the network.

There are several advantages to this system:

✦ The administrator controls which programs are used within the work group. Upgrading or adding new programs requires installation only on the server, not on each user's workstation.

✦ Since everyone's data files are in the same physical location, all those files are saved when the server is backed up. Users can also share data files when the files are in that common location. This, of course, is a requirement when multiple users are accessing the same database file simultaneously.

✦ Local systems don't need a hard disk. The boot and network files can be contained on one high-density floppy disk. By eliminating hard drives, you are removing the part of the computer system that fails most frequently.

✦ You can do away with local floppy disks entirely by adding special remote boot chips to the network cards. By eliminating floppy disks, you remove the risk of users copying program and data files from the network.

There are also disadvantages to relying totally on the server for program and data files:

5

+ If the server goes down (breaks), no one can do any work with his or her computer.

+ LAN versions of virtually all programs are required.

+ File access may be slower because the network traffic includes program and data files, as well as printer transmissions.

+ This arrangement is similar to the mini and mainframe setup, where all the power is concentrated in one location, the server/host. This returns you to "centralized" computing.

+ To provide reasonable response times to the many network requests, the server should be a very fast system with a very large hard disk. Even in a small network with seven users, that server might be a 386 33MHz with a 330MB hard drive.

Server Programs, Local Data Files

Another LAN design maintains the advantage of program control by locating all applications on the server but allows the users to keep data files on their local drives. The user accesses the server to load a program into the workstation. Once the program is loaded, the user selects data files from his or her local hard disk.

This design has some of the same advantages as the previous server program/server data file design:

+ The administrator controls all commonly used programs and versions.

+ Network traffic is reduced to programming load and printer transmissions.

There are, though, a number of disadvantages to this design.

+ LAN versions of the programs are required.

+ Workstations require hard drives for data storage. This creates more hardware that, in turn, may cause problems.

+ Each user is solely responsible for backing up their data files.

+ Data files cannot be shared between users on the network.

Since the workstations are equipped with hard drives, you can avoid the disadvantage of lost work time through server failure. If the local hard drives also contain copies of the program files, the loss of the network connection just means that the users switch to the local drives to load a local copy of the program. While the printer and other network resources are lost, the user may still continue to work. This contingency plan negates the advantage of having only one version of the programs located on the server.

Local Programs, Server Data Files

The previous design can also be reversed. Instead of the program files on the server and data being stored locally, the programs can be local and data files stored on the server.

There are several advantages to this design:

+ Keeping all the data files on the server provides consistent backups, assuming the server is backed up regularly.

+ Users can work with their preferred versions of programs on their local systems.

+ Users can share data files sequentially. Depending on the program, multiple-user access may be possible.

There are several disadvantages as well:

+ When the server goes down, the user cannot work with previously created data files.

+ Processing speed may be slowed with programs requiring constant access to the data.

+ There is no administrative control of the applications and versions.

In essence, apart from printer sharing, the server just provides more storage space for the users' data.

Local Programs, Local Data Files

The least complex network design leaves all program and data files on the local system. The network connection provides access to network printers and other resources, such as E-mail. This design produces the least disruption to the user's existing way of working with his or her system. If you decide to build the network plan in steps, this may be the best place to start.

This local control of all files has several advantages:

◆ Minimal disruption in the steps required to use programs and access data.

◆ Fast access of all files.

◆ Little effect on work when the server goes down.

There are, of course, a few disadvantages:

◆ There is no administrative control of the programs used to create the data files.

◆ Backups of data files must be initiated by the user.

◆ Data files cannot be shared between users on the network.

Mixed Design

Many networks use a mixture of the designs just described. Since most small networks grow from stand-alone systems to include the network connection, the design can grow as well. As mentioned, the easiest place to start is to leave all program and file access at the local level. But if you remain at that level, you may be missing some of the advantages of installing a network.

If you create your plan with several phases, you can more easily prepare your users for the transition. For example, the phases might be

1. Installation of the network and instruction on how to use the network printers.
2. Use of network E-mail to send phone messages and exchange files.

3. Implementation of a LAN version of the office word processing program.

Depending on your design, you can introduce the use of the server for data files at any point in the implementation. All of this might be scheduled over a two-month period.

Just these choices for the server/user files present a bewildering array. As you work through this chapter, you'll consider other factors that influence these choices. The following table summarizes the server design options:

Server	User
Programs/data files	None
Programs	Data files
Data files	Programs
None	Programs/data files

System Planning

If you have completed the planning worksheet in Chapter 4, you have a picture of your current setup. To continue the planning process, you need to consider specific elements in this picture. So far, the plan includes the following:

✦ All computers to be put on the LAN

✦ A sketch of the office layout with each computer's location

✦ An overlay including the cable paths and estimated cable lengths

✦ A potential location for the server

Using this and additional information, you'll begin to make decisions about your network. In each of these sections, common choices are included with additional possibilities covered in order of increasing complexity.

Selecting Software

The software selection is always the first place to start. Once the LAN software is chosen, the selection of network cards, topology, and cable type is narrowed down. When you select the LAN software, your general plan for program and data file locations helps determine which software you want to use.

If you want to have a LAN server that stores all the files, a dedicated server system makes the most sense. For example, NOVELL's NetWare 2.2 is designed for the high traffic required in that configuration. On the other end, if the file storage is to be split between the server and the workstation, a peer-to-peer system makes sense. In this case, Artisoft's LANtastic 4.1 or NOVELL's NetWare Lite 1.0 can provide those services.

In addition to the file storage, you'll want to create a list of other features you want in the software. If you use the notes from the worksheet in Chapter 2, you know what is important. If you want to use an E-mail system, you need to check the LAN software for that feature or make sure the E-mail program you want to use runs with the LAN software you are considering.

You must also make sure the LAN versions of the applications will run on the network you select. Contact the company or read the promotional information carefully for compatibility charts.

Where do you start? You can select the LAN software and see what else works with it, or you can select your critical application software programs and find a common network they all run on. In either case, making sure that each one of the software packages works with the other is a crucial step in the planning process, before you spend the first dollar on the network.

Network Cards for LAN Software

The network cards you select are dictated by the LAN software you choose. For small networks, many LAN programs use Ethernet cards. If all the systems to be connected are AT, 386, or 486 computers and each one has a 16-bit slot available, you can safely plan to purchase a 16-bit Ethernet card for each system.

TIP: Many network starter kits include the first two cards needed for the network. You may want to purchase just the starter kit for the first step in the installation. If those cards work, you can then purchase the additional cards for each machine from the same company.

If performance is not as critical and price is very important, you may decide to use ARCnet cards. Remember that, in theory, Ethernet runs as much as four times faster than ARCnet, while the difference in price may only be double.

If you have one or more XT systems or have only 8-bit card slots in some systems, you'll have to use the slower 8-bit card in those machines. You can use a mix of 8-bit and 16-bit cards on the same network. The systems with 8-bit cards will perform more slowly than those with the 16-bit cards.

Designating the Server

From your list of systems in the office, which is the most powerful? This would appear to be the logical choice for a dedicated server. But if you are designing a network that uses the server mainly to share a printer, provide E-mail, and exchange a few files, using the most powerful system in your office may be overkill.

If you are using a peer-to-peer system, the main server is likely to be used for other tasks. In this case, using the most powerful system makes more sense. Keep in mind, though, that with a peer-to-peer system, all systems can be configured as servers, distributing the workload across the LAN.

If you do not have a system readily available as the server, you may need to purchase one. Again, the tasks required can help determine how powerful the system should be. Remember that there is little need for a color VGA screen on a dedicated server. The most important consideration should be the size and speed of the hard disk, as well as the number of printer ports if you want more than one printer attached. Because this is a critical system, a dependable system (not the cheapest) is a high priority.

When deciding where to locate the server, consider physical security. The best way to prevent access is to lock the room containing the server. Of course, if the server location is in the boss's office, make sure you still have access when the boss is away.

Finding Network Printers

If the server is to have one or more printers attached, consider the location carefully. As mentioned in Chapter 2, the farther away the printer, the more time spent retrieving printouts.

A peer-to-peer system allows everyone to share the printers attached to their system. Maintaining the location of the printers when the network is installed saves some confusion for users. Users must also decide how to avoid disrupting each other when they retrieve printouts from other printers.

TIP: Watch the human traffic as users retrieve output from each other's printers. It may become obvious that those who produce the most output deserve the higher quality and quicker printers. The boss may also get tired of everyone coming in to retrieve printouts and be happy to move that laser printer to a more accessible location.

Also keep in mind the security of the actual hard copy. As with a fax machine, anyone can review the contents of the material being produced on the accessible network printer. The boss does not want to send the list of raises for the next quarter to this public printer. This consideration strengthens the need for individual printers in addition to the network printers.

Planning Cable Runs

The cable runs are the topology required by the LAN software. This is why a floor schematic is critical when planning the cable locations. This layout should also include possible electrical interference from large machines. If the cable is to be run across the ceiling, check for the location of the recessed lights, and plan to route cable around, not over, them. Also include any building code restrictions in the cable plan.

You must also know the limits for the length of cable. The signal becomes weaker as it travels down the length of the network cable. Your plan will easily show if you are trying to stretch your cables beyond the length recommended by the network card or LAN software companies. Those lengths are the maximums. If you stretch that maximum by just 50 feet, you can easily have intermittent problems on the LAN forever. If you must run cable beyond the maximum, use special devices called "repeaters" to strengthen the signal down the cable.

CAUTION: This bears repeating: *Do not* stretch the length of your cables beyond the maximum lengths recommended by the network card or LAN software companies.

User Considerations

You have considered the hardware and software issues related to planning this network. But if you leave your users out of the planning stages, you may create a network they don't want or need and won't use. Gather the users together and explain what you are planning. Ask for their ideas. Even if they express total confidence in your ability to handle the task, they will appreciate having been asked. They also will have no room to complain later if they don't like the results.

User Experience Influences Design

As mentioned elsewhere in this book, networks add new problems to the desktop computer environment. Consider each user's level of computer experience as you plan the network. How well does each user deal with a new problem? How much additional time should you plan on spending to provide help?

If most users on the proposed network rely on a menu to select their programs and have only a vague notion of what a directory is, you may want to concentrate the LAN in a dedicated server. If you put all programs and data files on that server, you maintain complete control, including user menus and program versions.

At the other extreme, if the majority of the work group is able to write batch files and each uses programs of his or her own choosing, the least restrictive LAN makes the most sense. In this case, the work group can be connected to the server and access whatever resources they have an interest in. At this level, they would be likely to operate a peer-to-peer system effectively, understanding how to "hop" from server to server to select and use each other's systems.

Perform a Task Analysis

Depending on how much you want to "entice" the users, you can describe all the possible resources available on the LAN. However, you may want to limit that list to the features more reasonably within your technical reach and budget. If you want to keep users interested, you can explain how everyone will be able to print to the laser printer and use the server to store files or for quick backup. You can also explain the E-mail system and how it might improve office communications.

This is also the time to brainstorm. How else might everyone work better when their desktop computers are connected? These ideas should be very specific, outlining the tasks within that group. The LAN will generally be useful for tasks shared between two or more users. As you identify specific projects, you can begin to develop a sense of directory structure. In addition to individual areas on the server, specific projects might also have unique subdirectories on the disk.

This task list also extends to single-user software that would be better run on a network. Determine if users exchange floppy disks with data. Does the data remain on the floppy disk because that is the master database? Would it be more efficient to have the database on the server and use the LAN version of the software to allow simultaneous updates?

Task analysis is an art and a science in itself. However, just listing the routine projects and tasks performed within the work group helps you plan the LAN effectively. You'll also get the users involved right from the start.

Providing User Training

Another way to keep users involved and satisfied is to provide them with training. In your plan, explain why the users need the training, what they will learn from the training, and when the training will be provided. This training may simply consist of a 15-minute explanation on how the network functions and how it changes the way the desktop computers will be used. Chapters 7 and 8 provide more ideas for user training. The point here is to make that training part of your plan.

Anticipating Growth

Your small LAN can grow in a number of ways. Your users may become more sophisticated, you may add more resources to the network, or you may need to add more workstations. Each of these possibilities should be included in the plan.

Even if most of your users rely strictly on the menu system someone created, don't assume this will always be the case. You cannot leave the network easily accessible because your users immediately head for lunch when confronted by the DOS prompt. Some day they may learn how to use the DOS command line. Or you may have an experienced computer user who begins work tomorrow. (If you have experienced users now, you definitely need to restrict access to some parts of the system.) In short, don't be lulled into a false sense of security because users are not able to cause problems now. You need to design a system with some open and some closed doors.

This growth in user experience is also likely to increase interest in adding resources to the network. Try to imagine and plan for these new software packages or hardware additions. This may mean purchasing a faster server because LAN traffic has slowed response times, or you may decide to standardize on the LAN version of most programs on your network. Looking ahead two years is reasonable. Within that time, a whole new generation of software and hardware products will have been introduced and you can begin planning again.

Part of the growth plan should include additional LAN stations. This may mean attaching existing desktop systems or purchasing new systems to add to the network. With the small network, this may mean growing from four to six workstations. With some software packages, you can add (and pay for) one station at a time. With other software packages, you purchase in the number of users by increments. If you plan to add two more users within six months, if may be more cost and time effective to purchase sofware now to anticipate that growth.

Playing Office Politics

Just as having the fastest computer or nicest printer confers status on the user, being connected to a LAN may also raise the status of a company or department. While this is not the best reason to install a LAN, you can make it work for you when dealing with your users. You can point out that not only are they using computers to perform their work, but they have multiplied their efforts by sharing the resources of a LAN. The more they cooperate in that effort, the more effective the LAN becomes. This mind-set may help you turn a reluctant group of users into "the few, the proud, the LAN users of Company B."

You may also have noticed that some users are not worried about status but still want the biggest toys. They want the fastest processor or software they don't need but want to "play with." As the local computer guru, you might have a slight tendency in this direction as well. Just keep in mind that you are not just talking about reallocating the resources within the LAN; you may be taking away someone's prized toy.

When considering this problem of redistribution, remember how your mother used to distract you with food when she needed to retrieve the crystal vase from your grubby little hands. The corporate equivalent might be a nice lunch or another piece of software to offset the need to shift the user's 386 to server duty.

Another unhappy fact of LANs, no matter how small, is that the LAN admininstrator asserts control over the users. Where computers were once personal, they've now been depersonalized, as indicated by such terms as "desktop computers" and "workstations." Some people might contend that this change of names is intentional; however, it's a simple fact that computer use is no longer personal when the user must rely on the LAN to accomplish his or her work.

Users can be controlled entirely when LANs are designed with all files located on the server. If you remove all local drives from the computers, the control is complete. Without the LAN administrator, the LAN does not function. If the LAN does not function, the users cannot do their work. Only the greatest need for security can justify this return to the centralized control of mainframes.

Hardware Limitations

Even the best LAN installation may come to a screeching halt if you have not considered the limitations of your hardware. The need to look at 8- and 16-bit card slots has been mentioned. The next most critical factor will be memory use in the individual workstations. A close second is the processing speed of each computer. Another hardware limitation includes the type of display.

5

Don't Forget Memory

Entire books have been written about memory and how it is used in desktop computers. If you are not at all familiar with standard, high, extended, and expanded memory, be prepared to learn about memory to optimize your LAN.

You can determine if memory resources are limited by examining the CONFIG.SYS and AUTOEXEC.BAT files for device drivers and TSRs. Use the MEM program in MS-DOS 5.0 or CHKDSK for other versions of DOS to determine how much of the 640K of memory is available from the DOS prompt. If the user has a lot of device drivers such as MOUSE.SYS and ANSI.SYS, there may not be enough memory left to squeeze in a large LAN program.

NOTE: "TSR" stands for "terminate-and-stay-resident." These are programs that run in the background while applications (what you see and work with) run in the foreground. Some programs install themselves as TSRs that you may not even know about, but they still take up memory.

You *must* know three memory values before you can be assured that your users can continue to work with their applications while connected to the LAN:

✦ How much memory is available from the DOS prompt?

✦ How much memory will the network software require?

✦ Will the user's normal applications run within that remaining amount of memory?

For example, if the MEM command indicates that 523K of memory is available from the DOS prompt and the LAN software requires 90K to run, the user has 433K of memory to operate application programs. If that is not enough, you'll have to consider different variables all along the line:

✦ Can you remove some device drivers from CONFIG.SYS?

✦ Can you remove some TSRs from AUTOEXEC.BAT?

✦ Can you select a LAN program that does not require as much memory to run?

The memory squeeze becomes less critical if your system has more than one megabyte of memory and you use memory-management software. Utility programs can help you map, study, and use this memory more effectively. The LAN software packages also provide ideas for more efficient memory management.

If you have any hint that you might run into memory problems, your first purchase might be a memory-management program. Learn how to use that program to maximize the available 640K of memory. Also look very closely at the different LAN programs' specifications for memory usage before you make your purchase.

Consider Performance

The workstation processor, the network card, the server hard disk speed, and the current traffic on the network affect the response time for network actions. While all of these factors have been covered elsewhere in this book, your planning document should consider their overall effect on the workstation's performance when using the network.

How long does it take to load a program from a local hard disk? If you are using a fast 386 and hard drive, the user hardly notices a delay between making the menu selection and seeing the program on the screen. This user will be much less tolerant of the delay when loading the program from the network than someone used to running programs from floppy disks. That one factor—program load delay—may discourage a user significantly when you declare that all programs are to be loaded from the server.

Even more critical in a multiuser environment is the delay between entering data and viewing the results. If both bookkeepers are used to entering data at different times on the same computer, they may be delighted to learn they can use the LAN for simultaneous updates. However, they may be very unhappy when they discover they must wait five seconds between entry screens.

The time delay between request and response is a common complaint of networks. Consider this when choosing the LAN software and how much traffic you expect. If the users must rely on the server for everything, you might want a more powerful network and server.

TIP: If you decide to work with a LAN consultant, make this response time part of the specifications. For example, under the highest load, the response delay will not be more than five seconds. Under the normal load, the response will be less than two seconds. The specifications would also include the programs and the current response times on the local machines.

Dealing with Screens

The different types of screens on the workstations will not influence your selection of the LAN software. LAN utility and menu programs are designed to use text for the display. The colors can also be changed for use on monochrome screens.

The different screen types, however, may be important with application software. LAN versions of this software can be configured to the individual's screen type and other preferences. The catch is that this configuration file must be accessed by the program when that particular user starts the application. That configuration file may be located either in the user's work area of the network or on the local hard disk.

If the workstations have different screens or you know users want custom settings for their applications, you need to plan for the location of those configuration files.

Allocating Network Resources

Once you have gathered the list of applications and made general decisions about the structure of the LAN, you can begin making more detailed plans. These decisions include the structure of the server directory and the type of access specific users will have to those directories.

Critical: Directory Design

Anyone who works at the DOS level has made directories (MD) and removed directories (RD). For some people, this process is ad hoc. They create and destroy directories without much planning. On a personal system, a user can get away with this lack of planning. On a LAN server, the directories must be thought out carefully. Making changes to the design affects everyone, taking hours of work and resulting in days of confusion.

Remember that the directory structure is like tree roots. Each root can contain one or more roots. When referring to a specific subdirectory, you can type each subdirectory name beginning with a backslash. For example, a subdirectory name might be \SHEETS\EXCEL\PROJECT. The PROJECT branch is under the EXCEL branch. The EXCEL branch is under the SHEETS branch.

The key to network use of these subdirectories is that you can assign a drive letter to a subdirectory at any point in the branch. You could designate the subdirectory \SHEETS\EXCEL as drive L on the network. When users access drive L, they see only the "L:" in the prompt. If they use DIR, they see all the files in the EXCEL directory and they see the subdirectory PROJECT. They could use the CD command to move into the PROJECT directory, at which point the prompt would be L:\PROJECT>. Notice that there is no way to move above the EXCEL subdirectory or even to know that drive L is actually \SHEETS\EXCEL.

Understanding this function of networks is essential when designing the server directories. How this connection is implemented may vary.

With NOVELL products, you use the MAP command. With products like LANtastic, the NET USE command accomplishes the same thing. The manuals provide the details, and the installation usually helps you set up those user drives. Your plan helps you prepare for the initial design. You can add more drives or make changes later if necessary.

In addition to this selective access of subdirectories, you can also designate how the user can work with the files in that subdirectory. The types of access levels vary in LAN programs. All LAN programs include the ability to restrict access to "read only" so that users can load the program files but cannot erase or save files to that subdirectory on the server. "Write" access must be available for a user to write data files to the server's hard drive.

5

A sample directory structure is shown in Figure 5-1. The programs are all contained in one branch and the user work areas are contained in another. The program branch would be "read only" for users. Each user would have a drive that pointed directly to his or her subdirectory.

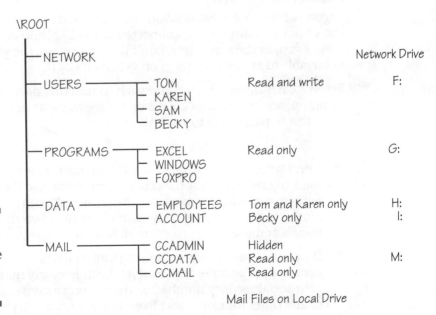

A sample directory structure for the server

Figure 5-1.

Planning Security

Security planning is an essential part of a network. As long as you think about restricting access at each step, you can make the network more secure without making it more difficult to use. Some of the security methods include good directory design, effective passwords, and restricting physical access.

Directory Restrictions

As mentioned in the section entitled "Anticipating Growth" earlier in this chapter, LAN security is always an issue. Even if you are confident that you can trust everyone, you cannot always trust everyone to know exactly what he or she is doing on the network. A properly designed directory tree will help keep users from accessing the wrong directories and modifying files. Carefully check all users' access levels to make sure they cannot move into restricted areas or modify the wrong files.

Password Security

Logon passwords are essential on any LAN. Without passwords, anyone can sit down at any system connected to the LAN and access that user's files. If you, as the supervisor, don't use a password, the system is vulnerable to anyone who logs on as SUPERVISOR.

Everyone has his or her own approach to selecting passwords. The most common, and worst, is to use his or her logon name or initials. Here are some tips to pass along to the LAN users:

✦ Don't write the password down! If you must write something down, use a trigger word, not the actual word. If you use the word "mom" as your reminder, for example, the password might be your mother's maiden name. Or you might write down someone else's initials and use that person's middle name as the password.

✦ Don't use your first name, a nickname, your initials, your children's names, a pet's name, any relative's birthdate, any numbers from your social security number, or your phone extension. QWER, ASDF or any other four keys next to each other on the keyboard are commonly used as passwords, and you should avoid these as well.

♦ Password ideas: a child's middle name, a favorite movie, a city you would like to visit, a favorite song, a company you once worked for, or the name of a summer camp you once attended.

♦ The best password consists of two unrelated words separated by a punctuation mark. For example, "ocean&vegetable" would provide a higher level of password security because these words have no connection to each other or to you.

Some LAN software allows you to set the number of days between password changes. For instance, every 30 days the system might require users to change their passwords immediately after they log on to the network. Some systems do not even allow previously used passwords to be repeated. You need to include these parameters in your network plan if this level of security is important to your organization.

Physical Security

A dedicated server should be locked away from everyone. This provides the highest level of physical security for the network. Of course, you may have to compromise on this restriction if you also have printers located next to the server.

TIP: If the server is nondedicated (that is, if you can also use it to run applications), do not have the server automatically log on as SUPERVISOR. If you do, anyone with physical access to the server has access to the entire system.

Preparing the Plan

There are lots of ways to prepare the plan. The following worksheet provides some ideas for the forms you might use. Add to these forms as you discover the information. Then use the checklists at the end of the chapter to see if you have each part of the plan completed.

User Needs

Start with the users. List the tasks they perform on a regular and occasional basis. List their storage needs and the optimum printer for the hard copy. The user design sheet could include this information:

User Needs Worksheet

Name: _____

System used: _____

Computer task: _____

Program used: _____   Memory required: _____

Storage: ___Temporary   ___Permanent   ___Shared with
Output: ___Laser   ___Letterhead   ___Color
                ___Continuous feed   ___Standard   ___Wide

Computer task: _____

Program used: _____   Memory required: _____

Storage: ___Temporary   ___Permanent   ___Shared with
Output: ___Laser   ___Letterhead   ___Color
                ___Continuous feed   ___Standard   ___Wide

Computer task: _____

Program used: _____   Memory required: _____

Storage: ___Temporary   ___Permanent   ___Shared with
Output: ___Laser   ___Letterhead   ___Color
                ___Continuous feed   ___Standard   ___Wide

Desktop Computer

Each system to be attached to the LAN needs to be inventoried as well.

System type:

___XT/8088 ___AT/80286 ___80386/80486

Display:

___Mono ___CGA ___MCGA ___EGA ___VGA

5

Printer: _____

Memory at DOS prompt: _____

Slot open:

___8-bit ___16-bit ___EISA ___MCA

Current user: _____

Checklist: Phase 1

You have gathered a lot of information. So far, you should have the following:

◆ Your reasons for creating the network (Chapter 1)

◆ The advantages the network will provide (Chapter 2)

◆ A decision as to whether you will install the network (Chapter 3)

◆ A list of all the equipment you have

◆ A sketch of the office layout, with stations and wiring

◆ An estimate of the distances from station to station

◆ A completed survey of users' needs

Checklist: Phase 2

List all the software used in the work group (from the user survey) on another sheet. Determine if there is a LAN version, which LAN software it is compatible with, and how much memory is needed at the workstation. Address each category that follows for every application used in the work group.

Program: _____

Version: _____

LAN Y/N: _____

Memory: _____

Cost per user: _____

Cost of upgrading: _____

Checklist: Phase 3

Now you need to make some preliminary decisions about the LAN design. Use pencil. These decisions will change as you discover other factors in the network.

The first decision is the file locations:

	Server	User
___	Programs/Data Files	None
___	Programs	Data Files
___	Data Files	Programs
___	None	Programs/Data Files

The second decision is the server base:

___Peer-to-peer   ___Nondedicated   ___Dedicated

The third decision is the network type:

___ARCnet   ___Ethernet   ___Other

The fourth decision is the cable type:

___Twisted-pair   ___Coaxial

5

Checklist: Phase 4

Begin examining the various LAN software programs available. Purchase one of the major computer magazines and examine the ads. Call and talk with the company about your requirements. Visit other LAN sites. Compile information on the LAN packages you are considering:

Program name: _____

Company: _____

Cost per user: _____

Server requirements: _____

Workstation memory used:_____

Network card types:_____

Cable types: _____

First Draft of the Plan

You can work forward from the LAN versions of the application software you want to run. Alternatively, you can select the LAN software and then determine if your applications are compatible. Once everything looks settled, use the following checklist to build your first draft of your plan:

___ The LAN selected

___ Network protocol and cable type

___ A list of additional hardware and software

___ A cable routing and workstation location sketch

___ A timetable for implementation of each phase, including installation, testing, and user training

___ A sketch of the directory structure on the server(s)

___ A list of "things users should know" about the network

As you continue with this book, you may find new factors that influence your decisions. This is a planning document. Changes are almost guaranteed.

Summary

This chapter has provided an example of how *not* to install a LAN. The most noticeable problems came from a lack of planning. The remainder of the chapter has provided additional elements to be considered in the process of creating the plan:

✦ All files can be located on a server or can remain on the workstation.

✦ If the focus is on a server-based LAN, examine the LAN versions of the application programs you want to use. If users depend on the

LAN just for printer sharing and E-mail, you can start with the LAN software and look for the features you like.

+ The distance between the workstations and routing for the cables may influence your decision on the LAN software.

+ You need to talk with your users as you work on your plan.

+ Resources may need to be redistributed if office politics allow it.

+ Memory and speed limitations may affect the LAN software choice.

+ Security on, and for, the network is always an issue.

5

CHAPTER

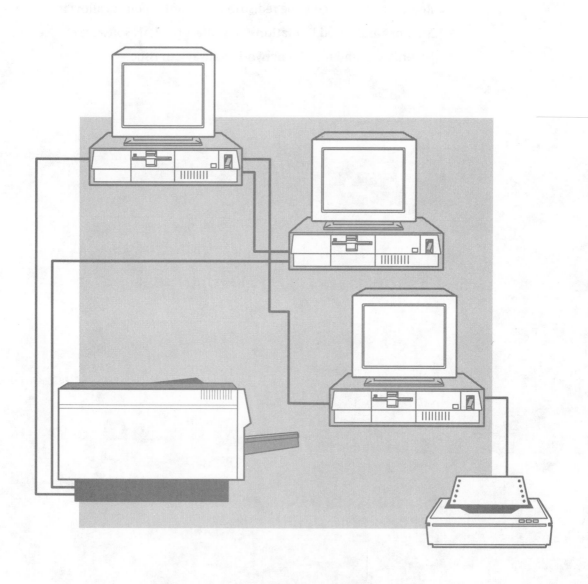

INSTALLING NETWORK HARDWARE

Once you have completed the first draft of your network plan, you need to know how to install the physical parts of the network. These parts include the cards and the cable. The cable can be run over walls, through walls, or just across the room. Installing network cards also takes some patience. A checklist at the end of this chapter helps you prepare to install cards and make cable connections.

Installing network cards, cables, and connectors need not be any more difficult than installing the LAN software. The keys are to check your work each step of the way and use the right tools. This chapter provides information to help you install the network cards and cable connectors and ideas for running the network cable.

If you follow a few safety rules, you won't damage anything. The worst that can happen is the installation won't work. The best that can happen is the hardware works and you are ready to install the software.

Preparing for the Installation

Time and energy spent preparing for the job saves time and frustration while working on the job. There is nothing more discouraging than halting a project midway because you don't have the right tools. Without the right tools, the result is sloppy, unreliable, and possibly dangerous. Preparing for the job includes knowing the basic rules of safety to protect yourself and the equipment, as well as making sure you have the proper tools. And don't imagine that you must complete the entire project in one day, regardless of how small or large your LAN.

Observing Safety Rules

Above all, you must be aware of basic electrical safety rules when working with hardware. Electronic devices are sensitive to electricity, especially the nuisance of static electricity. For example, as you insert a card into the system, the static electricity in your body can travel through, and may damage, the card. Listed here are a few basic rules. Additional tips are included with each step of the hardware installation process.

+ Always allow a system to become completely quiet after turning it off and before moving it. The hard disk is vulnerable to damage while it is still spinning.

+ Always unplug any electrical device before removing any covers. Just turning off the power switch does not disconnect the system from the electrical current.

6

✦ Never consume liquids around an opened device. If, in the heat of the moment, you are sweating profusely, stop to wipe your brow. One drop of that salt water inside the computer could damage it.

✦ Always touch a grounded object before picking up a computer card or reaching inside the system.

✦ Leave the card in the protective antistatic plastic pouch until just before you need to use it. If you must make changes to the switches or jumpers on the card, lay it on top of the plastic bag, which you have placed on a flat surface.

✦ Always use the right type and size tools. If you use a power screwdriver, be very careful not to overtighten screws.

✦ If you drop a screw inside the case, stop and immediately retrieve it. If you forget to get it and turn the system on later, you could seriously damage the computer.

✦ When working around electrical wire, be careful not to route network cable near or over the wire.

✦ When cutting holes in wallboard, be very careful not to cut into electrical wire or plumbing.

Hardware installation can be very physically demanding. You may be moving systems around and climbing ladders. You will definitely be removing covers and bending over as you insert the cards. Remember to take it easy. The physical activity may increase your frustration level.

If you are doing the installation during nonworking hours, you may want to talk someone into assisting, even if that person doesn't know the business end of a screwdriver. Sometimes it helps to have someone to talk with as you work through the problems you encounter.

Securing the Necessary Tools

Before you take the first step of the installation, prepare as you would for performing surgery—place all the instruments within reach. Then, when you need a specific tool, you can just reach for it. Don't use a flathead screwdriver to remove a screw just because you can't easily reach the Phillips screwdriver. Computer toolkits are widely available at computer stores and are well worth the $25 or so.

Keep in mind that you'll need different types of tools for installing cards and for installing cable. Here's a list of tools you might need to install a network card:

◆ Four screwdrivers—a small and medium size of both flathead and Phillips. Better yet, secure a series of hex head drivers if your systems have hex head screws.

◆ Find something to extract screws dropped inside the computer. A medical clamp called a hemostat is handy. A doubled-up piece of sticky tape on the eraser of a pencil will also do.

◆ A small flashlight is useful as you peer down into the innards of the computer, especially if you are digging around for a dropped screw. A small, plastic flashlight is better than a large metal one in case you drop it into the computer.

◆ A small mirror will help you see behind the system if you don't have the space to pull it out from the wall or can't bend over far enough to see the ports in back.

◆ A power screwdriver saves time when removing and replacing screws in the back of the system. Remember to keep a loose grip to prevent overtightening the screws. If you use the power screwdriver to remove and install the screws that keep the cards in, be very gentle.

◆ A small hair dryer is handy for blowing out dust in the system.

◆ Small needle-nose pliers help move card jumpers.

The tool list for installing cable is a bit more lengthy. Not only must you cut the cable, you must also strip off parts of insulation and then properly clamp the cable connector, such as a BNC or RJ-45, on the end of the cable.

◆ Be sure you have the proper crimp for the connector you are using. The crimp looks like a strange set of pliers. Depending on the quality and the specific tool, it may cost from $20 to $100. If you are making BNC connectors, this tool is essential. If you are using twisted-wire (RJ-45), there is a way to avoid making cable connectors, as noted in the section "Using Twisted-pair Connectors" later in this chapter.

◆ Get and use large, sharp wire clippers.

◆ Find a sharp knife to cut away insulation. Better yet, there are wire strippers that will cut the insulation to the exact measurements you need before attaching the BNC connectors. The $50 is well worth the savings of time and greater accuracy if you are making more than four or six cable ends.

◆ If you will be going through walls, find a drill with a long 1/4-inch by 6-inch bit.

◆ A small ball of string with a weight tied at one end is essential for pulling cable across suspended ceilings.

◆ Use wide masking tape or blank mailing labels to mark cable ends.

◆ Borrow two tall ladders if you are running cable across the suspended ceiling tiles.

◆ Find a small keyhole saw if you need to make access holes in the wall.

◆ If the suspended ceiling has insulation, you and anyone working with you need gloves and a breathing filter.

With the exception of the cable crimp and wire stripper, the tools just described are readily available. The cable crimp and wire stripper should be available from the same source as your network cable and connectors. Make sure you get the proper crimp size for the BNC connectors and cable.

Selecting Test Systems

If you purchased a LAN starter system, you already have the software, two cards, and the proper type of cable with connectors. This cable may be from 15 to 25 feet long. Even if that is not long enough for one of your connections in the network, it is exactly what you need for the first phase of your installation.

One of the most useful and time-saving steps you can take is to move two systems next to each other, as shown in Figure 6-1, for the first part of the network installation. In most cases, bring another system as close as possible to the server. You'll use these two systems at the same time

Two systems
next to each
other for testing
Figure 6-1.

to test both the server installation and the workstation's ability to access the server.

With the two systems side by side, install the first two cards, install the server, and then install the workstation. As you test and smooth out the process, you just shift from keyboard to keyboard like a pianist playing a duet on two pianos. This beats running down the hall two dozen times to the nearest station to see if the server is working and if the workstation has made the connection.

As you would with any computer, make sure this temporary arrangement includes a sturdy table for the second system. You may need another power strip if the receptacles are taken up by the server. Since you will have 15 to 25 feet of slack in the cable, avoid heavily traveled areas where coworkers could easily trip.

Installing Network Cards

Above all, before installing the network cards, read the accompanying documentation. With luck, you won't have any surprises. Those surprises occur when you have two cards trying to use the same settings. In most cases, the default settings on the card will work. Try those settings. If they do not work, you'll find out about it fairly quickly and can worry about those finer points later.

Make sure you have located and written down the technical support number. (Lack of technical support is a drawback when doing the installation on the weekend.) Find the page in the documentation that shows the specifications, including the I/O base address and the IRQ (defined in the section "Network Card Problems" later in this chapter). If all goes well, you won't need this information. If you need to change some settings, it will be important.

Installation Steps

You should install any new computer part slowly and carefully. The smaller the changes, the less work you have to undo when problems arise. Here are the steps you should follow. (More details are provided after this list.)

1. Turn on the computer to make sure it works.
2. Turn it off, unplug it, and remove the cover. (Remember to allow the system to become quiet after turning it off and before proceeding further.)
3. Gently blow out any dust.
4. Locate an empty slot in the motherboard.
5. Remove the mounting bracket from the back of the system.
6. Touch grounded metal to discharge static electricity.
7. Remove the card from the antistatic plastic bag.
8. Insert the card.
9. Plug the system back in and turn it on. (The cover is still off.)
10. Test the card.
11. Test the system.
12. If you have problems, turn off the system and study the next section, "Network Card Problems."
13. Install the LAN software.
14. Turn off the system. Replace the slot screw.
15. Replace the cover of the system.

Here are the details. Turn on the computer to make sure it works. Run through a few of the main programs. Make sure the mouse works if you have one. If a printer is attached, make sure it prints. If there is a modem, check that as well. There is always the chance that something was not working correctly before you installed the network card. It is maddening to try to fix a problem that you think was caused by the card but was actually present before the card was installed; checking the system beforehand eliminates that possibility.

Once you are satisfied that the system works as expected, turn it off, wait until it is completely quiet, and then unplug it. You can disconnect it from the wall or from the back of the system. Remove the cover by unscrewing all the screws around the edge of the back. The cover may have to slide all the way forward before you can lift it off. Some covers just slide forward an inch or so and then lift off. Keep the cover screws together in a safe place.

If no maintenance has been performed on the system within the past six months to a year, you'll have an accumulation of dust. Use the hair dryer or other gentle blower to push the dust out of the system. A vacuum is not recommended; nor is blowing with your moist breath.

In the motherboard, locate the slot for the network card, using your flashlight if necessary. Make sure the slot has sections if you are installing a 16-bit network card. If it doesn't, you must install an 8-bit card or, alternatively, move an 8-bit card from a 16-bit slot into this currently open 8-bit slot, thereby opening up a 16-bit slot.

Remove the mounting bracket, shown here, by unscrewing the small screw at the top of the back opening in the case:

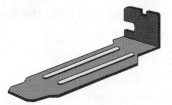

As you loosen the screw, hold it carefully so you don't have to fish it out of the system later. Keep the screw handy, but save the mounting bracket somewhere else.

Touch grounded metal to discharge static electricity. Then stand very still while you reach for the network card.

Remove the card from the antistatic plastic bag. Lay the card on top of the bag if you need to make any adjustments to the jumpers or dip switches. (See the following section, "Network Card Problems.")

The slots on the motherboard have small spring contact strips that match the contact strips on the bottom of the card. As you insert the card, you may have to rock the card back and forth (not side to side) very gently to get it all the way into the slot. The mounting bracket on the card should be exactly at the top edge of the system back support. Do not use excessive force to insert the card. You might damage the network card or motherboard.

If you knew for sure the card would work, you could just put the cover back on. But there is a chance that the card will conflict with other cards in the system and you may need to make changes on the card. With the cover still off, turn the system back on. Be very careful here. You have an open system with power in it. Anything you touch or drop into this open system could damage you, the system, or both.

If there is a major problem, you might get extra beeps or the system may not boot up. The odds of this happening are slim, but possible. If this occurs, refer to the next section of this chapter. If the system starts normally, you are ready to test the card. Most card manufacturers provide a disk with utility software, including a program to test the card. Refer to your card's documentation for the name of that program and then run it.

If the card test program runs, then try using the major software programs installed on the system. This step is essential because if you don't and you load the LAN software, you won't know if the problem is with the card or the LAN software. Make sure you test the mouse, the printer(s), and the modem by running programs that use these devices.

If you had problems with your network card or application software test, turn off the system and unplug the cord again. Then refer to the next section of this chapter.

If you did not find any problems, install the LAN software for the server or workstation. You need not worry about setting up the entire

6

directory tree. (Refer to Chapter 7 for more information about this part of the network installation.)

If no problems were noted, turn off the system and unplug the cord. The temptation may be to just replace the system cover, leaving out the network card retaining screw while the power is on. *Don't!* The screw must be replaced in the network card, especially because the cable pulls on the card. Attempting to do this work with the power on is very hazardous.

With the power still off, replace the cover of the system. If you use a power screwdriver, be sure you don't overtighten the screws in the back.

Once you've installed one network card, don't assume that the installation will be the same for all the other systems. The only way this occurs is if all the systems are exactly the same brand, have the same cards, and use the same software. If you bought the computer systems one or two at a time, even from the same manufacturer, there may be different problems.

The only difference on the second system, temporarily sitting next to the server, is that the software you install will be for a workstation, not a server. Even if you plan to make each system a server in a peer-to-peer scheme, start out with the simplest configuration and make this system a workstation. You can change the installation settings later. Also keep in mind that when you attempt to start the workstation software for the first time, it will not complete the process until the two systems are attached with the network cable.

Network Card Problems

Network card manufacturers try to create card settings that work in the majority of computers. If you have a system with one serial port (COM1), one parallel port (LPT1), and no unusual cards, there is a good chance the default settings will work. On the other hand, if you have a CD-ROM drive, a second serial port, a music or some other special card, the network card may have the same settings already used by one of those devices.

Most network installation manuals provide suggestions to resolve conflicts between the network card and other cards in the system. Those recommendations include changing dip switches and moving jumpers.

Dip switches are small sets of usually eight switches. By setting these switches on and off in different combinations, you create a setting for the system and software to use as a reference. The manual should show the numbers used for these settings. Make sure you know the on and off positions on the block. Use any small pointed device to move the switches. Here is an illustration of dip switches on a network card:

You may also have to move jumpers on the cards. These *jumpers* are small plastic blocks that fit over two metal pins. The inside of the jumper contains metal. When the jumper covers two pins, it closes the circuit, creating another setting on the network card. In many cases, there will be two rows of pins with four or five pairs. A jumper is to cover only one pair of pins. Here is a set of pins with one jumper:

6

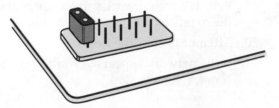

Most network cards have just one set of dip switches although there may be many sets of jumper pins. The network manual will have a drawing of the card with the different pin locations and names. On some cards, the settings are also printed next to the pins. Use the needle-nose pliers to gently pull the jumper off the current pair of pins, and then push the jumper back on the new set of pins with your finger. However, before making changes to these settings, sketch the original location of the jumpers and dip switches. If you continue to make changes, make a new sketch for each setting. Also write down the value for that setting.

When you make changes to the card, you'll also make changes to the network software. The whole purpose of making these changes is to avoid conflicts with other cards in the system. Since the network software must be told those new settings on the card, you'll need to reinstall the software or make changes on the command lines contained in the CONFIG.SYS or batch file used to start the network.

Making changes in the card settings to resolve conflicts can be a very tedious process. You should make only one change at a time in the card. Two changes at the same time might cause additional problems. To make and test changes, follow these steps:

1. Make sure the system is off and unplugged.
2. Touch grounded metal to discharge static.
3. Gently rock the card out of the slot.
4. Place the card on the antistatic bag.
5. Sketch the current dip switch or jumper setting.
6. Make the change on the card.
7. Insert the card back into the system.
8. Plug in and power up.
9. Reinstall the network software or make the changes in the batch file to reflect the new card setting.
10. Attempt to start the network.
11. If the network appears to work, continue to test your applications. If not, return to step 1.

Another effective but time-consuming approach to resolving conflicts is to remove all the nonessential cards in your system, leaving only the video, disk drive, and network cards. If the network card works, you then add cards one at a time (with the power off, of course) until you locate the card causing the conflict. This information is very helpful for anyone providing technical support.

The number of possible settings and conflicts may seem overwhelming. Your ability to solve the problem depends on your perseverance and technical support. As noted in Chapter 3, there are many sources for help. Don't be reluctant to begin working down your list, starting with the network card tech support phone number.

The longer you wait, the more upset you may be with yourself if the solution takes 30 seconds to explain. The tech support person might say, "Oh yes, we've seen that problem. Just move the jumper J4 to J5. This sets the card to a nonstandard bus." You may not know why this works, but you may have wasted two hours searching in vain for a solution available in one phone call. Keep in mind that the response might also be, "Gee, I'm not sure. I've never heard that one before. Have you tried changing the settings on the network card?"

As do all cards, the network card uses a number of settings to work within computers. These settings include the I/O port address, the interrupt requests (IRQs), the base memory address, and other settings, and they are a major reason why you might have problems with the network card installation. This is because no two cards in a computer can use the same IRQ, DMA, or I/O port address. While it is not essential that you know how these settings work, understanding the basics may help you try different values to get your network card to work.

The methods used to change these settings may differ. Older cards use physical methods, described in detail in the next sections. Newer cards, though, may make these changes with software. You run the special software program to make the changes once the card is plugged in. Those new settings are then saved on the card. You can run the software again to make further changes.

The I/O Port Address

Each card in the system has a unique I/O port address. Many of these are reserved for specific types of cards, such as the video card. For example, you can't have two VGA display cards in the same system. Other card addresses are not unique to the card type. Network cards, as well as other cards, fall within this category. This is why these cards have dip switches to change the I/O address.

Any "extra" cards in the system, such as a CD-ROM, music, speech input or output, digitizer, or scanner card, may already be using the default setting on the network card. If you have one or more of these cards, you'll need the documentation for these cards to determine that setting. If that card works correctly, you are better off making changes to the network card instead.

The possible addresses for network cards range from 2E0h to 380h. The dip switches can be set either ON (0) or OFF (1). With eight positions, that number expresses a binary number from 0000 0000 to 1111 1111, or 0 to 255 decimal. The catch is that the numbers used to represent the I/O address are in hexadecimal. Therefore, the number 300h is represented as 0011 1111 on the switches. You need not know hex to make the changes, but you must make sure your switch settings match those in the network card manual.

TIP: The small "h" after the numbers indicates that the number is in hexadecimal, also referred to as hex. This is a numbering system organized on base 16 instead of base 10 (which is what the decimal system uses). The manuals show the hex number and the switch settings. You may need to insert that hex number in the network settings. When you do, don't include the "h" as part of the number.

Change the settings on the network card and software to a unique I/O address. If it still does not work, return the address to the original setting and consider changing the IRQ.

Interrupts (IRQs)

While the I/O address represents a unique ID to the computer, the interrupts are used to get the computer's attention. When the card needs to send something to, or through, the system, it "interrupts" the current processing. The system then checks the card to process that task.

The IRQs (interrupt requests) range from IRQ0 to IRQ15. As with the unique I/O, the interrupts also need to be allocated, one per card or action. The standard interrupts include IRQ4 for COM1 and IRQ3 for COM2. If you have an LPT2 port in your system, the IRQ5 is also being used. In most cases, though, the IRQ5 is a good choice if you have both COM1 and COM2 in your system. You can try the IRQ2, but this interrupt may not work well in 286 or faster systems.

On most cards, you change the interrupt by moving a jumper. One row of pins on the card represents all the IRQ settings the card can use. Some network cards have just three settings, while newer cards may have five or more pairs of pins. As with the I/O addresses, you'll have to check the IRQs used by other cards for potential conflicts.

Base Memory Address

The network card contains its own memory to buffer the transactions on the network cable. This must "fit" within the memory addresses that DOS can use. The network card memory fits in the reserved memory between 640K and 1024K, called high DOS memory. The common settings for network cards include C000h, D000h and D800h.

Just like the I/O address and IRQs, this setting must be unique in the computer. For example, EGA and VGA display cards and some hard disk controller cards use the area starting at C000h. You'll use another set of jumper pins to change the base address if you have conflicts here.

Other Settings

Network cards have even more settings. These include the DMA (direct memory address), the channel, the cable type, the node address, the remote boot PROM, and the reconfiguration timeout, and they rarely need to be changed. Make changes to these settings only if advised by tech support or with specific directions from the network card manual.

Making Cable Connectors

Once you have installed two network cards, you are ready to connect them with a cable. If you purchased a network kit, typically you get one cable section already made. You can use this cable to test your network with one server and one workstation. Once you are satisfied that you have the beginnings of a network, you can run the cables and make the permanent connections.

Even before you begin tossing cables, you need to know what you must do to attach the cables. As mentioned, make sure you have the proper tools to make reliable connections.

Installing BNC Connectors

You use BNC connectors for network coax cable. Make sure you have the specific BNC connector for the cable size. The connector sleeve is crimped to hold the connector to the cable. If the connector is too large, the cables come apart. If the connector is too small, the coax cannot slide inside the connector.

6

When purchasing the cable and connectors, get specifications for the amount of insulation to trim. These measurements are very important for proper contact between the cable and connector. Figure 6-2 shows a typical diagram.

The actual BNC connector kit contains three pieces. The smallest piece, the tip, covers the inner wire of the cable. The second and largest part is the actual twist connector. The third piece is the sleeve. This sleeve slips over the cable insulation and clamps the cable to the end of the twist connector. The following illustration shows these pieces:

Making a cable connector requires some practice. Cable connectors are not that expensive. You may want to take a few feet of cable and a few connectors and sit down to practice. This practice time helps later when you are in a rush to see if the whole LAN works. These are the steps for making a connector (more details are provided after this list):

1. Cut the cable, allowing several feet of slack.
2. Trim the insulation.
3. Insert the sleeve on the cable.
4. Attach the tip and crimp.
5. Slide the connector on the cable.
6. Bring the sleeve up and crimp.
7. Tug on the connection to test its strength.

Here are the details. Make a clean cut of the cable with heavy-duty wire cutters. If the end gets smashed or hacked off with a knife, the connector is much harder to attach.

Using the guide, trim the insulation to the exact measurements. As mentioned, if you want to make the cleanest and most accurate trims,

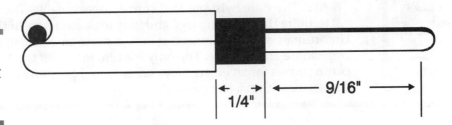

A trim diagram for a specific cable and BNC connector
Figure 6-2.

purchase a cable trimmer. If not, use a very sharp knife. Do not try to use generic cable-stripping pliers. Work over a piece of paper; the braided portion of the cable sheds tiny wires as you trim it.

Insert the sleeve on the cable and move it up the cable a foot or so. If you forget this step now, you'll work to get the main connector on the cable and then have to take it off again to put on the sleeve.

Attach the tip and use the crimp to flatten the bottom end slightly. The crimper tool has a special area for this purpose. This assures good contact between the wire and the tip.

Slide the connector on the cable, making sure there is some overlap of the insulation and braided wire. How much overlaps depends on the size of the cable and the sleeve. The more overlap, the stronger the connection.

Move the sleeve up and over the end of the connector. The sleeve should touch the bottom of the connector and cover part of the insulation. Use the crimping tool to squeeze the sleeve, insulation, and braid against the end of the connector. Some crimpers create a six-sided crimp; others produce two edges on the sleeve.

Tug on the connection to test its strength. If it wiggles, seems loose, or comes off in your hand, cut the whole thing off and try again. Do *not* try to repair your first attempt. Weak connections in network cable will eventually drive you to despair.

Making solid BNC connectors is a real skill. As long as you accept the fact that you will need practice and you'll make a mess of the first few, you can do it.

TIP: There are twist-on BNC connectors available. They do not require the crimping tool and may look attractive to the beginner. Unfortunately, these connectors *always* cause trouble later on; they come loose and corrode. The only legitimate use for twist-on BNC connectors is for an emergency connection. Make sure to replace that connector within a few days.

Using Twisted-pair Connectors

With the RJ-45 twisted-pair cable connectors, you have eight wires to handle. You must strip the insulation from the cable without cutting the inside wires. Each wire must then be inserted in the proper slot in the plastic connector and then crimped with the special tool. If one wire is crossed or is not crimped properly, you may spend hours tracking the problem to that source.

The better approach when working with twisted-pair cable is to purchase the cables with connectors already made from the wire supply vendor. You then run the cable connector from the computer to a receptacle you've installed in the wall. The receptacles are easy to wire because they use screw-down connections. You strip the insulation, wrap the wire around the post, and screw it down.

Other Connection Methods

The RJ-45 and BNC connectors are the most common for small networks. If you decide to have someone run the cable and make the connections, listen carefully to the method that person suggests. The cable and connector companies constantly improve their products and the ways to use them.

Do keep in mind that the more exotic methods are also likely to be the most expensive. Make the vendor propose at least two quotes, one based on the most recent technology and the other using less expensive, tried-and-true technology.

Running Cable

Getting cable across an expanse of space is variously called tossing, pulling, stretching, stringing, or running cable. Each word describes the method used to install the cable. The most common ways to run cable for a small network are to toss it through the suspended ceiling or pull it through the walls.

Even before you decide if you are going to toss or pull cable, you need to consider whether or not you need help with this part of your network project.

When to Get Help Running Cable

Fire and building codes exist as safety measures for occupants of all buildings. When you begin using space outside the normal working rooms, you are affecting the construction of that building. One of the best and most serious reasons to get help with your cabling project is to work with someone who knows the building codes. An electrician experienced with network cable knows what kind of cable the building requires. Not only can the electricians do the hard physical labor, they'll make sure the cable is properly routed to avoid interference and potential breaks.

Before you hire electricians to do the cabling, make sure they have experience and understand the limitations of the medium. For example, they might proclaim that they always leave an extra 20 feet of cable coiled up in the ceiling—"After all, you never know when you'll need it." This potential vendor does not understand the limitations imposed by network cable.

In some situations, placing the cable will just be beyond the capabilities of a novice cable installer. These situations require special tools and expertise, and might include the following:

✦ Workstations on two or more floors in the building.

✦ Cable layouts exceed the rated length and require repeaters.

✦ Building code requires special installation.

✦ Your company has strict work rules.

✦ The cable must be installed through duct work.

✦ You want network outlets in the walls.

✦ The cable must be pulled through cable conduits.

When looking for a contractor, remember that you can supply the cable and finish the connectors yourself; some LAN specialists mark up the cost of cable 200 percent or more and may want to charge $6 to $10 per connection. You will want the contractor to tag the ends of each cable and test for continuity before he or she is finished.

If you install the cable yourself, you'll need at least one other person to help. Someone needs to be on the receiving end as you pull the cable from one spot to another. When working on ladders and around electrical equipment, it is also a good idea to have two people working together in the event of an accident.

Running Cable Over Ceilings

Network cable is commonly laid across the top of suspended ceilings. If you've never poked your head up into a suspended ceiling, you'll discover that you are not the first to use this area of the building. You'll find air conditioning ducts, phone cable, electrical wiring, and the top part of the recessed lights in the ceiling. The heavy items such as the duct work have suspension wires from the support beams, just like the frames for the ceiling tiles. Other cables may just be lying on top of the ceiling tiles. Depending on your building code, this is also how you will install your network cable.

Your basic strategy is to lift the ceiling tiles every 15 to 20 feet between point A and point B. You then toss a weighted string from hole to hole. The better your aim and the fewer objects in your way, the further apart these access holes can be. Once the string has completed the route, you tie and tape the cable to one end and carefully pull the cable from point A to point B.

Ceiling tiles are made only to absorb sound, not to support much weight from above. Most tiles are made of pressed fiber and can be easily broken by hand. Don't lean on a tile from above and don't place anything heavier than a few coils of cable on the tiles.

You must be very careful when you push a tile up for access. Always push at one end. If that end resists, try the other. If that end will not lift, something may have been routed over that tile that prevents it from moving. Move your ladder one tile over and try again.

Once the tile lifts up, you may be able to shift it over or tilt it up to provide access. There may or may not be additional insulation on top of the tile. If there is, you should wear long sleeves, gloves, and a breathing mask. The material in the insulation is very irritating to your skin and respiratory tract.

Based on line of sight, open another hole in the ceiling about 15 feet away. Assuming you have a helper, stand as far up as you can in the first hole and toss a small weight with string attached toward your helper in the other access hole. The likelihood of success with each toss depends on how much space you have between the suspended ceiling and the real ceiling, how many objects are in the way and how large they are, your throwing accuracy, and your partner's willingness to stretch in all directions.

The actual weight on the string is not critical. It just needs to be heavy enough to carry the string for a 20-foot toss. The string should be attached to the weight so there is nothing to catch on other objects when you pull the weight back toward you. You'll miss your target once or twice and will have to try again. You may want to bring several weights in case you tangle the string so badly that you have to cut that section off and start again with another weight. A casting weight for fishing works well, as shown here:

Once you reach your first intermediate access hole, continue to open new access locations and toss to each successive hole. You may want to leave the tiles open to inspect the cable as you pull it through the ceiling. If the cable appears to have a very clear path, you could replace the tile, saving yourself a trip back later with the ladder after the cable is pulled.

Just tying the string to the cable is not enough. Wrap a piece of wide tape over both the cable and string, as shown here:

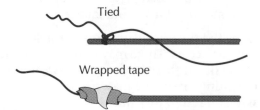

This helps prevent the end of the cable from becoming caught on another wire as you pull the cable through. Duct (gray) tape or wide masking tape works well.

You may also find fire walls if you are running cable from one part of the building to another. These walls are typically concrete and extend to the roof. You'll have to route the cable through the access holes already provided for other types of cables. Try to avoid routing through a hole also containing electrical wiring. Also, if you're using twisted-pair cable, be careful to avoid fluorescent lights and electric motors that can cause interference.

Depending on the cable type, you may need to pull two sections of cable through the ceiling. For example, most of the workstation locations may be on a thin Ethernet cable path. But one office may be enough off the path that you have to run the cable to and from that office. You need not toss the string twice. Before you pull the cable through with the string from point A to point B, attach the end of the string to the cable so you pull both the cable and another section of string. You can then use that second section of string to pull the second cable back from point B.

If you are routing the cable across the ceiling, you have to decide if you want the wires running down the wall. If building code prohibits it, you have no choice. If you want to hide the wires, you'll spend additional time cutting an access hole in the bottom of the wall. Again, depending on the latitude in the building code, you may be able to just leave the access hole, or you may have to install a cable receptacle. (As noted in the discussion of twisted-pair cable, a receptacle is a good idea.) Use the keyhole saw to create the opening, watching carefully for electrical wire in the wall. Drop the weighted string inside the top of the wall until you can grab the string through the access hole. Pull the cable down the wall just as you did when pulling it across the ceiling.

If you choose to leave the cable outside the wall, you can minimize its distracting presence by using a corner of the room, especially if the corner is behind a door. You can also use cable tie-downs with self-adhesive pads to hold the cable in place against the wall. Use a minimum number because when removed, the adhesive tends to remove paint and wallboard. Here is one type of self-adhesive cable tie-down:

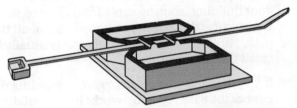

The ceiling tile must still be replaced to restrict air flow into the room. You can use a sharp knife to trim a small notch in the tile, just big enough to let the cable through. Or you can break off a corner of the tile to leave enough extra room to bring the cable through. Don't try to bend the cable to go between the edge of the ceiling tile and the suspension frame. That kind of sharp turn is likely to damage the cable.

Running Cable Through Walls

If the offices containing the workstations are next to each other, you may be able to route the cable through the wall. Most office walls consist of two layers of fiber or plaster wallboard, separated by aluminum or wood studs. With a 1/4-inch-wide, 6-inch-long drill bit, you can easily drill a hole in a corner of the room. While there is little chance that the electrical cable runs to the corner, extreme caution is suggested. If, after the bit goes through the first layer, it hits something before reaching the second layer, quit drilling immediately. If it did not hit electrical wire, it might be water or drain pipes.

Installing cable through the walls may be a bit tricky and is a method more likely to require a professional installer. But if your route is through plaster walls and without the complication of concrete or metal, you'll require less cable and won't have the problem of cable hanging from the ceiling. Again, check your building codes and the local work rules before you drag out that 6-inch drill bit and begin poking holes in the office walls.

Other Routes for Cable

Running cable throughout buildings is an important consideration in the building's construction. Designers also recognize the need to add cable later and provide conduits and access areas for telephone, power, security, fire alarms, and other types of cable. Depending on the age of your building, routing cable from floor to floor may not be too difficult. But because this requires a knowledge of all the other cables in the path, this kind of cable installation is usually beyond the abilities of a small LAN installer.

If you do need to cross floors, your building owner may have a contractor who regularly works in the building. If the building's contractor does not know how to run network cable, you may have to pay the extra expense of teaming up the contractor with a network specialist.

Testing Connections

If you like to measure success in small pieces, you may want to run a section of cable, install the connectors, attach it to the network card in the workstation, and see if it works. With some Ethernet networks, remember to move the terminator cap to each successive station as you build your network section by section. This method helps you locate a problem system or cable run immediately.

Other installers place all the cable, put on all the connectors, attach all the systems, and bring up the LAN, all at once. This approach is more dramatic and arguably more efficient for a professional installer. If you like this approach, you'll have to use a process of elimination to discover any problems you have.

In all cases, make sure there are no systems powered on and attached to the network when you work on cable or attach another station. (This caution applies to attaching or detaching anything to or from a computer.) If you use the "try each connection" approach, you must turn off all the systems on the network before making further connections. You then need only turn on the server to test the latest connection. You then turn on the other workstations, one at a time, to make sure each one works. With larger networks, this connection-by-connection method would add a lot of time to the installation process. With your small network, the time is justified because you will know immediately where a problem is.

You'll also want to complete extensive software testing. This process is covered in detail in Chapter 7.

Network Card and Cable Installation Checklist

As you prepare for your first physical LAN encounter, you want to be prepared. Use the following checklist to determine your state of readiness.

6

___Completed network plan in hand with cable routing sketches

___Helper standing by

___Complete collection of tools, including ladders

___All supplies necessary

___List of phone numbers and support people

___An extra pocketful of patience and perseverance

Summary

This chapter shifts the small network from the planning to the hardware installation stage. Chances for success depend on careful planning, following basic safety rules, and plenty of patience. Snagging a helper who has worked with network cable wouldn't hurt either. In this chapter you discovered the following:

- ✦ Safety first.
- ✦ Use the right tools for the job.
- ✦ Setting up a two-station version of your LAN is good practice for the real thing.
- ✦ Test systems before and after installing network cards.
- ✦ Installing cable is hard work.
- ✦ You are more likely to need professional help with the hardware part of the LAN installation.
- ✦ Go slow and test as much as you can.

CHAPTER

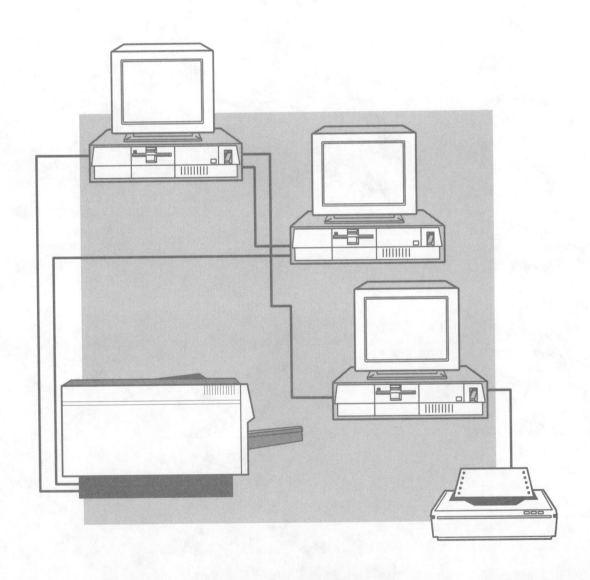

7

SOFTWARE INSTALLATION

After the physical parts of the network are arranged, you'll install the network software for the server and workstations. A two-station arrangement helps significantly for those first tentative network connections. You can test the connections and make changes without running back and forth between the server and one station. A checklist at the end of the chapter provides helpful pre- and post-installation steps for you to follow.

Chapter 6 covered the hardware installation and stated that installing the network hardware need not be any more difficult than installing the LAN software. This is not to imply that installing network software is necessarily easy. You'll need to take your time and be prepared for any number of problems. The more complete your plan, the better chance you have of successfully installing a small network.

This chapter covers the typical steps for software installation and testing that first connection. Once that test works, you'll organize the server and set up the network resources and accounts. Specific software programs are discussed for each of the general applications originally mentioned in Chapter 2. User training is highlighted at the end of the chapter.

The information in this chapter is based on several network programs, including NOVELL's NetWare Lite, NetWare 2.2, and Artisoft's LANtastic 4.1. While specific steps and commands used in the installation process are covered, they are provided simply to supply background information. The actual procedures you'll use to install your network program of choice will be detailed in that program's manual. In addition, the application programs covered provide a perspective on just one of dozens of choices in each category.

Preparing to Install LAN Software

Successful installation of any software requires a good understanding of the computer, careful reading of the manual, and time to test the results. You must know the computer because, in many cases, you must tell the software how to configure itself. For example, you may need to know the type of printer, the COM port with the mouse, and the type of monitor attached to the system. With network software, you need to know the card settings, the printer ports in use, all the user names, and other facts. With the information gathered in previous chapters, you should be ready for your installation.

The manuals can range from one 160-page book with NOVELL NetWare Lite, to four manuals with Artisoft LANtastic, to over ten pounds of manuals with NOVELL NetWare 2.2. The number of manuals reflects the complexity of the software. While you need not read everything in the manuals, you should read the basic installation instructions and have an idea of the contents of the other manuals. The larger NOVELL

NetWare package even contains a four-page guide to help you decide where to start in the stack of manuals.

Leave yourself plenty of time for the software installation. No matter how long you think the installation will take, it will take longer. Installing software is not just copying files to the hard disk; it's also making sure the resulting software works. Thorough testing always takes days and it is too often left to the users to discover the problems. The longer you spend testing, the fewer problems your users will experience. Fewer problems result in a higher level of confidence and a willingness to use the network effectively.

Also note that some programs modify the CONFIG.SYS and AUTOEXEC.BAT files. In most cases, it is easier to let the program put the proper settings in those files. Before you begin the installation, make copies of those files to another disk. If the network installation does fail, you can restore those files back to the root directory. You can also study the old and new CONFIG.SYS and AUTOEXEC.BAT files to determine exactly what the network software changed.

CAUTION: Some LAN software programs start by erasing your hard disk. You must have backup copies of files to restore the hard disk once the server software has been installed. Even with peer-to-peer networks, making a complete backup of the server hard drive before starting the installation is essential.

7

Running a Test Installation

It's okay if this is your first time inserting cards and running cable, but you should be familiar with installing software before you attempt to install LAN software. The inevitable trial-and-error method of solving problems requires a reasonable amount of experience with software installation.

As recommended in Chapter 6, the first step is to arrange two systems side by side for the installation of the server and one workstation. You can use your network plan to begin setting up the server as you make the installation choices. If you are really prepared, you have already arranged the directories on the server to conform to your network plan. Don't try to answer all the installation questions at first. Just set up the minimum to get the two systems to communicate. You can then work back and forth between these two systems as you build the network according to your plan.

Installing the Server

The first step for any software installation is to make copies of the disks supplied with the program. Make these the working copies—label them and use them for the actual installation. Store the originals in a safe place.

To begin the installation, you'll typically insert the first disk in a disk drive and type **Install** or whatever program name is provided in the network manual. From there, the installation program will ask questions or provide a screen of settings. Once you have answered the questions or changed the settings to suit yourself, the program continues by copying the proper files to your hard disk. The specific responses you provide affect the command-line settings and the initial defaults. Figure 7-1 shows the main installation screen from the Artisoft LANtastic 4.1 installation program.

While the questions for your network may not be presented in the same order or using exactly the same terms, the concepts will be the

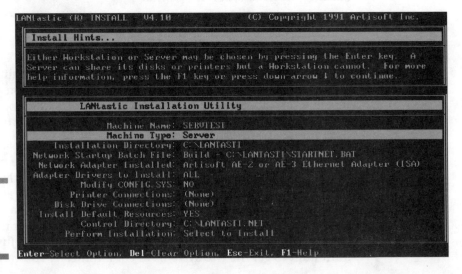

The LANtastic installation screen

Figure 7-1.

same for all LAN installations. The information you supply on this screen represents many of the decisions you make while installing the network software. Remember that this installation may take several attempts before it works the way you want. Make changes now, while you are in the test phase, and not later, when you have users depending on the network.

The more complicated programs, such as NetWare 2.2, may use eight or more disks and start the server installation process by reformatting your hard drive. This step alone can easily take an hour or more. When working with these more complicated programs, you need to allow even more time to try different settings.

Machine Name

Every system attached to the network must have a unique name (the machine name). Using your network plan, you name the main server something like SERVER or HOST01. If you will have more than one server on the network, try to make each server name reflect the function of that server. For example, the accounting system might be ACCTSERV and the main server might be MAINSERV. Once other workstations begin using the network, this name cannot be changed easily.

Machine Type

There will be only two choices for the machine type: the installation will either be for a server or a workstation. Make sure this setting is "server" for the first installation. Remember too that the server can also be a workstation in peer-to-peer networks. With a single-server network, the additional choice might be whether or not the server is also to be used as a workstation—a nondedicated server.

Installation Directory

Some installation software allows you to specify the directory the network files are copied into. In most cases, you should select the default directory name provided. The installation software will create the directory and place all the files within it. The selection of this directory affects other settings created by the installation program as well—usually the path and startup batch file commands.

Startup Batch File

Network programs create a batch file with all the commands and switches necessary to start the network. The default STARTNET.BAT is reasonably easy to remember, although it may be created in the network directory and won't work unless you move into that directory first. In most cases, you'll incorporate that batch file into your AUTOEXEC.BAT file or call STARTNET.BAT from the AUTOEXEC.BAT file. Here is the STARTNET.BAT file created by LANtastic:

```
@ECHO OFF
PATH C:\LANTASTI;%PATH%
AEX IRQ=15 IOBASE=300 VERBOSE
AILANBIO
REDIR DAN LOGINS=3

NET LOGIN/WAIT \\HOST DAN
NET USE F \\HOST\C-DRIVE
NET USE LPT1 \\HOST\@LASER
NET USE LPT2 \\HOST\@DOTMATR
NET LPT TIMEOUT 10
```

TIP: The startup batch file is also the best place to study the sequence of commands used to start the network. If you are having trouble, you can print the file and then use that listing to type each command separately. This process can help you identify which part of the network startup process is causing trouble.

Network Card and Drivers

The network software must be configured for the specific network card. If you purchased the LAN as a kit, those choices will be minimal. If you purchased the software separate from the network cards, you may have a long list of cards to select from. If the card you have installed in the computer does not appear on your list, the drivers may have been supplied by the card manufacturer. You may also need to call the card vendor to see if their card has an equivalent on the network installation list.

Printer Connections

Naming the printer connection is the first step in setting up the network resources. This prepares the server to share that resource by establishing the printer port to use, such as LPT1 or LPT2. The name you assign is just a convenient way to remember the printer attached to that port. If you have two printers, a laser on LPT1 and a dot matrix on LPT2, it makes the LAN easier to use if you name these resources LASER and DOTMATR instead of PRINTER1 and PRINTER2.

TIP: The network does not need to know what kind of printer is attached to it. It routes the printer data only through the server. Your LAN or local application software must still be configured for the exact type of printer attached to the network.

Defining Resources on the Server

7

Remember that each device to be shared across the network is called a resource. Your network plan determined what those resources were to be and what names to use. When you are setting up accounts, this information will be critical in providing the resources each specific user needs. In the first part of the server installation, you named those resources. Now you must allow those resources to be shared on the network. When first installing the server, you may want to just set drive C as a resource. This provides access to anything on that drive, a condition you want only when first testing the server. Later you will limit access to specific areas on the hard drive for file security.

You allow a drive or specific subdirectory to be used by expressing the full path and then applying a name to that subdirectory. You do this in different ways with different LAN programs, but once done, it allows users to access those resources by providing the full server name of the resource and then assigning a local drive or printer port. For example, the resource you could have named ACCOUNT is actually C:\DATA\ACCOUNT on the server. To the user, it just becomes drive L.

Drive Connections

If the server were to be linked to other servers on the network, the drive connection area of the installation screen would contain one or more entries. If you eventually set up a number of servers on your peer-to-peer network, each server is likely to have drive connections with other servers. This entry becomes very important when installing a workstation.

Control Directory

The control directory stores the information for user accounts and resource information. Because this is a critical setting, the default provided by the installation program is recommended.

Other Server Settings

Once you install the LAN software, you'll have additional tasks, such as creating user accounts and managing the print spooler. These tasks are covered in more detail in Chapter 8.

Installing the First Workstation

In a peer-to-peer system, the installation software is the same for each workstation. You'll create a unique name for each workstation, just as you did for the server. The big difference will be that you specify WORKSTATION instead of SERVER for the machine type. Once you make that change, several others become more important.

With server-based software such as NetWare 2.2, the user installation requires different software, but the questions and concepts remain essentially the same.

The Printer Connection

Since the workstation may also be using a local printer, you need to tell the installation program which ports already have a printer attached and which ports will be redirected to the remote printers. For example, LPT1 might already have a printer attached. You might then set LPT2 as the printer on the server. To the user and the application software, the workstation has two printers, one on LPT1 and the second on LPT2. The network software then controls the redirection of the LPT2 printer data.

Drive Connections

Setting up the drive connection is critical for the workstation. If you are in a test phase, you may just select a server drive resource such as C-DRIVE as your drive F. Once drive F is installed in the STARTNET.BAT file, the workstation sees it as the drive and directory named C-DRIVE. If C-DRIVE is the same as C:\ on the server, the workstation drive F has access to the entire hard disk drive C. The following table shows this relationship:

Network Name	Actual Directory	Workstation Drive
C-DRIVE	C:\	F
ACCOUNT	C:\DATA\ACCOUNT	L
MAIL	C:\CCMAIL	M
VICKI	C:\USERS\VICKI	G

Testing the First Two Systems

7

Once you have the workstation software installed, you are ready to test the network. Because the network installation software may have changed the CONFIG.SYS file, reboot the server and the workstation. Then run the network batch file, possibly named STARTNET, assuming you haven't already made it part of the AUTOEXEC.BAT file. Run the server STARTNET first so the workstation can connect to the server.

If all goes well, you'll have additional drive letters and additional printers from the workstation. Depending on the software, you may have to log onto a network drive before you can do much with the server. For example, with NetWare 2.2, you'll need to log on as SUPERVISOR. This gives you total control of the network. Or you may need to run NET_MGR in LANtastic to set up the first user account. The requirements of this first step must be extracted from the network manual.

If all does not go well, you may have one or any number of problems to handle. In most cases, you'll need to dig into the network manuals to find ideas. Here are a few common problems with possible solutions:

No Network Drive   Drive F is the most commonly used drive letter for the first network drive. If there is no drive F, try other drive letters.

You may have specified another starting drive when installing the software. Another possibility is that the network did not start at all. In this case, you'll probably see error messages from the network batch file.

Can't Log On   If you do have the network drive but can't seem to do much with it except look at the directory, you may not be logged on. As mentioned, this differs among networks. With NOVELL networks, the logon name of SUPERVISOR provides system-wide access. With LANtastic, you'll need to run NET_MGR from the server to create your first user account. Then you can log on under that account name from the workstation.

Server Not Found   When the workstation first boots, it looks for a server by name. If you have changed the name of the server or entered a different server name when installing the workstation software, the workstation cannot locate the server by name. Check the server name on both the server and the workstation logon script. Also make sure the connectors on the cable are firmly attached to the cable and the network cards.

System Locks Up   If the system locks up, you may have a conflict with the hardware or with other TSR software on your system. These steps may help you to isolate the problem:

1. Use the network test software to make sure the card is functioning. If it is, continue. If not, return to Chapter 6.
2. Create a boot floppy disk that loads just the bare minimum in CONFIG.SYS. Determine this by examining the CONFIG.SYS file created by your network installation.
3. Boot from this "clean" floppy.
4. Try the network batch file from the hard disk.
5. If the system does not lock up, you know something loaded as a device in CONFIG.SYS or as a program running as a TSR in AUTOEXEC.BAT is causing the trouble. You'll have to add each line in the CONFIG.SYS and AUTOEXEC.BAT files one at a time to determine where the problem is.

Network Card Not Found   The network software may run but be unable to locate the network card address. Check to see that the card address matches the address in the startup batch file. Use another network card in this machine to see if that solves the problem. If you have only two cards, swap them and see if the problem follows the card or stays with the computer.

Finishing the LAN Installation

Now that you have made the first test connection, you are ready to configure the server to suit your network plan. This includes creating user and group accounts, creating user work areas (if necessary), assigning additional resources, and testing the applications to be used on the server if it is also to function as a workstation.

User Accounts

You control the user's access to the network's resources via the user account. The network supervisor (you) creates accounts that can include the user's name, a description of the user, a password, hours and days access is allowed, special access privileges, and more. This data is important for keeping track of the many users on the network and to prevent users from accessing files in other users' areas.

As supervisor, you must set up an account before that user can access a server. On a peer-to-peer system, a specific individual's name must be in the user account file in order to access the resources of that server. This is how the local supervisor at a server/workstation controls access to the resources on his or her system. To remove access, the supervisor of that server deletes the user's name. Chapter 8 also covers the maintenance of user accounts.

Group Accounts

With LANtastic, group accounts have all the features associated with a user account. You can set up a group account to be used by a number of people at one time. For example, if three people in marketing need exactly the same access to programs and files, you could create a group account named MARKET and allow those users to log on as MARKET. You could then restrict network access to areas only the marketing department needed to use.

7

NetWare 2.2 uses groups in another way. For example, when the network is first installed, all users are automatically made members of a group named EVERYONE. The group contains access to the network subdirectories necessary to run the network. You can create and name additional groups with different access areas and resources. Once the group is created, including that group name in an individual user account gives that user all the same settings as the group.

User Work Areas

If you intend to have users save files on the server, you should create specific areas on the directory for each user. For example, you might create \USERS on the server and then create \USERS\BILL, \USERS\VICKI, and \USERS\DIANE. Each user would have his or her own directory on the server. This directory would appear to the user as a drive letter. For example, what the user sees as G:\ is actually C:\USERS\VICKI on the server.

The users can access that area on the hard disk just as though it were a local drive. They can make, change, and remove subdirectories and save and delete files. This disk space may appear to be limitless to them. Chapter 8 provides some suggestions for managing user work areas.

Finishing Resource Installation

If you plan to reorganize your server hard drive, this is the time to do it. Using your network plan, you should create directories, move files, and do whatever it takes to create the planned directory structure. If you have enough hard disk space, you can simply copy files from one directory to another and then delete the files in the first directory.

If you have a lot of directory and file rearranging to do, you may want to consider a utility program such as Central Point's PC Tools 7.1. One of the many functions in this program is directory pruning and grafting. With this feature, you can select and move entire directories, with all files intact, at one time.

Completing the installation also includes setting up your additional resources, such as the fax board, the CD-ROM drives, or other devices. Test those as carefully as you can before you turn the users loose on the network. These are even more delicate to install and manage than the network software.

Testing the Applications

If you plan to also use the server as a workstation, test the applications you plan to run on it. These applications, probably left over from the pre-server hard drive configuration, must be able to run at the same time that the server software is running. The server software requires more memory and "steals" processor time. Once the server and workstation software are loaded, you may not have enough memory to run the applications you intend to run. If this is the case, you'll need to look into a memory manager program and possibly purchase more memory.

If the applications run too slowly on the server/workstation, you may need to change the network plan and allow that computer to function just as a server. The alternative is to accept the loss of speed. You'll also need to test the performance later when users begin accessing the server, which slows down the speed even further.

7

Installing the Remaining Workstations

When setting up the remaining workstations, you may discover differences that affect the network cards and the network installation software. Be prepared to solve a whole new set of problems with each workstation connection. The only exception to this rule is if all the computers are exactly the same.

There are several approaches to actually getting the network software on the additional workstations. You can use the original network software and answer all the installation questions again. Or to save time, you can copy the network files from the first workstation to subsequent ones. With a few exceptions, those files from the first workstation will be exactly the same on the remaining workstations.

The first exception occurs if you changed any of the settings on the network card. If you have, you'll have to make changes to the startup switches in the STARTNET batch file on the new workstation. If you installed the card with the default settings, you do not need to make any changes.

The second exception applies to all the workstations. Since each user must log on with a unique name, the command-line parameters must be modified for that user's name. For example, LANtastic uses NET LOGIN \\SERVER\USERNAME. Each workstation batch file must have a unique USERNAME. If the network startup batch file does not include the logon, then this does not need to be modified, although you may want to include the logon command as part of the startup batch file for the workstation users.

A final exception occurs if the network software is purchased one user at a time, such as NetWare Lite. Each of these disks has a unique number and must be installed on only one machine.

Testing the LAN

At this point in the LAN installation, you may have spent a long day or more installing cable, inserting cards, copying software, and testing the LAN connections. You may be ready to declare the network operational and go celebrate—but don't. If you want to earn even a modicum of trust from your users, you'll spend more time testing the applications on the LAN.

While you cannot begin to simulate all the possible conditions that can occur on a network, you can attempt a few. As you went from station to station and tested the LAN, each may have worked well. But the purpose of a network is to handle multiple actions. With one or more assistants, you need to put the network under some kind of load. This includes loading files at the same time you use the network printer. Use a database with the file on the server while someone else loads a file. Try as many combinations as you can think of.

Don't have the extra time? Too many network installations leave out this last step or reduce it to a 15-minute test drive. This puts the users in the position of testing the network. These are the people you want to use and benefit from the network. Do as much as you can. If you also want to let your users know what you tried, make a short list of these tests and provide a copy. Even if some of these combinations subsequently fail, the users will know that you considered the situation and that it appeared to work at the time.

As you'll quickly discover, the users will create many different combinations, some of which will result in problems. If you have provided an adequate orientation for the users and can offer a reasonable response to their problems, the users should be able to see the network as another way to extend their computer processing power.

Installing LAN Application Software

If the server is to contain program files for multiple users, you need to purchase the LAN version of your application software or test the single-user version very carefully. Keep in mind that newer programs may not be designated as LAN versions but may still be "network aware" and can share files across the network. For example, Borland's SideKick 2.0 is a personal calendar and utility program. While the program package does not state "LAN version," the third paragraph on the first page explains that the program allows files to be shared across a network. In this case, a group calendar can easily be kept on the network for everyone to access.

Installing LAN application software may not be any more complicated than installing any software. On the other hand, there may be a few additional considerations or problems that develop during and after the installation. The following sections provide a thumbnail sketch of several applications to illustrate the installation steps. These examples provide a quick idea of what installing this type of software may involve on a LAN.

7

Basic Installations

As with any software installation, you need to remember the basics:

✦ Install from backup copies or at least write-protect the originals.

✦ Make sure you have enough disk space before beginning the installation.

✦ Know your equipment well enough to answer any installation questions.

✦ Make backup copies of the AUTOEXEC.BAT and CONFIG.SYS files prior to installation.

✦ Send in the registration card.

Network software requires some additional precautions and steps:

✦ Install the program files in an accessible area on the server.

✦ Make that area read-only to prevent accidental deletions.

✦ Provide an area for each user's configuration files.

Each LAN or network-aware program has its own requirements. While you may not always read the manual when installing single-user software, the potential for multiple problems with multiple users suggests the need to read the LAN manual.

Also note that some of the applications discussed here may already be included in the LAN software you select. For example, LANtastic has a small mail program and can access a CD-ROM drive on the network. As always, you need to evaluate the features offered in each package to determine if that program, or another, would best serve the needs of users on the network.

CD-ROM Drives

Using a CD-ROM as a resource across the network may require special software, depending on the type of LAN. One program you can use with NOVELL NetWare 2.2 is CD Connection from CBIS. The program provides up to 21 CD-ROM drives on a network, contained in a dedicated CD-ROM server. A major advantage of this dedicated CD-ROM server is that CD-ROM device (SYS) drivers need not be loaded on the local workstations.

The CD Connection manual contains a number of sections, each devoted to a specific network product. There is a 21-page section for NOVELL networks that includes a checklist, both quick and extended installation guidelines, and tips to fine-tune the CD server. Installation of additional programs on the workstation allows access to the CD-ROM server on the network.

Installing this software requires an understanding of CD-ROM drives. The CD-ROM drive should have been tested first on the local system.

An extensive knowledge of device drivers and the ability to modify the CONFIG.SYS file are also required. Access to the CD-ROM is not limited to the number of users; it is limited only by the availability of the network resource.

Communications

A popular communications program, Procomm Plus, produced by Datastorm, also has a LAN version. This allows multiple users to access a modem in another system. The five-user package includes five complete manuals, a feature not typical for most LAN programs.

This product requires an additional program in the NetWare environment before it can be used. The NOVELL ACS (asynchronous communications server) software must be installed before Procomm Plus LAN can be used. NOVELL ACS requires a dedicated server containing one or more modems attached to a NOVELL NetWare 3.1 network. This example demonstrates the need to know the software's requirements before purchasing for the network.

7

Electronic Mail

cc:Mail from Lotus is a very popular electronic mail program for networks of all sizes. The software comes in a basic platform package for DOS, Windows, Macintosh, and other operating systems. The platform program creates the post office and provides the user interface. You can add additional users in increments of 8 or 25. Additional cc:Mail programs, such as Gateway, allow transmittal of messages from server to server and through a modem.

The software installation is relatively easy for someone familiar with the concepts of E-mail. As the system administrator you must establish a post office and set up individual users. All the mail messages are kept in one location on the server, with password-protected access for each user. Users can be notified when new mail arrives in their mailboxes and access the messages from within other applications. Figure 7-2 shows the menu screen for cc:Mail.

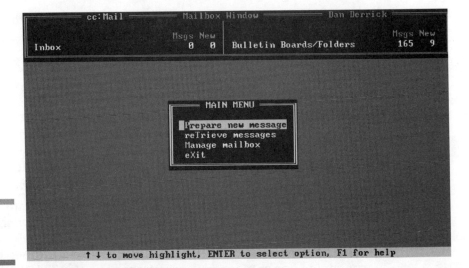

The cc:Mail
main menu
Figure 7-2.

Windows

Microsoft Windows 3.1 provides a popular interface for newer, more
powerful systems. It uses graphic images (icons) to represent programs
and files making access easier and more intuitive. The user may not
even know whether the files are located on the local directory or a
network directory.

Windows is very efficient on a network. When it is installed on the
server, all the files are copied to the Windows subdirectory. When it is
installed on a workstation from the server, only the files required to
start Windows locally are copied to the local drive. When additional
programs are needed from the server, Windows accesses those shared
files. The user's data and files can be kept on the local drive.

Windows requires fast 386 systems with at least 4MB of memory. This
latest version, 3.1, is very stable and very network aware. Installation to
the server takes some time and a considerable amount of disk space.
This translates into minimal time to set up workstations and minimal
local disk space used. Figure 7-3 shows the network dialog box for
Windows.

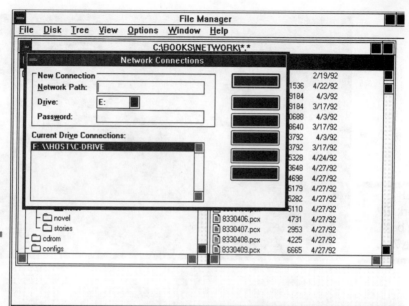

The Windows
network dialog
box
Figure 7-3.

7

Basic Databases

Database programs, such as PC-FILE 6.5 for LAN, are "basic" only
because they do not include a programming language. They still have
all the features you need to manage large files of data. The LAN version
provides record locking, an essential feature required when more than
one person uses a database at a time. This expands the individual
management of a database to the group level on the network.

The documentation includes a separate booklet explaining how the
LAN version is different from the single-user version. It explains the
minimal differences and changes necessary to adjust for various
networks. The network booklet also provides a clear explanation of
record and file locking. Figure 7-4 shows the network user ID dialog
box, which identifies everyone using the same database.

PC-FILE
network ID
dialog box
Figure 7-4.

Programmable Databases

Programmable databases, such as dBASE IV version 1.5 from Borland,
provide all the features in a basic database program, as well as a
programming language. With this language, a programmer can
completely control the use of the data on the network, including the
required file and record locking. But these programs can also be written
to guide the user through the process of adding and editing data and
printing specific reports.

dBASE IV provides individual LAN Packs to be used on the network.
Each package contains a dBASE manual and a disk to increase the
number of users able to access the program on the network. With this
method, a copy of the single-user version is installed on the server.
Then, for each additional user access, the LAN Pack software is run to
increase the count on the server copy. For every disk from each
additional LAN pack, the user access count is increased by one. For
example, the purchase of dBASE IV and three LAN Packs allows four
users to share one database at a time.

User Training

Your network planning document should include user training as one of the several steps to a successful network installation. The administrator of a small network has the advantage of keeping directly in touch with all the potential users. If the users have been part of the planning process, they already know something about the network. Additional training will help them learn the details and help you when you have to solve problems.

Training Basics

Arrange the user training as soon as possible after the network has been installed. Better yet, provide basic instructions even before the network is active, and then follow up with a problem-solving session. Here are some additional ideas about the training:

◆ Announce the specific times for training as far in advance as possible. This allows everyone to work around that established date.

◆ If possible, provide the session away from the office. If this is not possible, don't allow interruptions during the training session.

◆ Encourage attendance by providing a meal or other incentive.

◆ Sessions should involve management, even if they are not using the network directly.

◆ Provide handouts geared to the users on the network. Always include a summary of commands on one sheet.

◆ Limit sessions to four hours. Most information provided after four hours is lost in the mental cobwebs.

7

Training Outline

The training details vary with the users' level of experience and how much they really need to know. The training you provide will be based on your network design. For example, the results of a server crash affect the users differently if everyone depends on the server for files than if they just use it for printing. A training outline for a three-hour orientation might look like the following.

Three-hour Training Session Outline

I. Definition of a LAN
   A. PC-to-PC connections
   B. Server(s)
   C. Workstations
   D. Cable connections

II. Advantages
   A. Sharing printers
   B. More hard disk space
   C. LAN software (upgrades)
   D. Multiple access to data files
   E. File backup

III. Disadvantages
   A. More problems
   B. Server crash
   C. Additional expense

IV. Differences in the workstation operation
   A. Memory limitations
   B. File access times
   C. Use of additional drives
   D. Use of additional printers
   E. New applications available:
      1. E-mail
      2. Backup
      3. Group calendar

V. Typical problems
   A. Out of memory
   B. Printer conflicts

Three-hour Training Session Outline

      C. Server crash

      D. Problem-solving steps

      E. Whom to call for help

  VI. Access levels

      A. Directories as drives

      B. Read-only

      C. Full access

  VII. Privacy

      A. Supervisor's access

      B. E-mail messages

      C. Company policy

7

Problem Solving

A LAN training session provides an opportunity to review with users the basic steps for problem solving. While being covered as part of the network training, these steps apply to any problem associated with computers. These are the three Rs of problem solving: Recover, Report, and Re-create.

Recover from the Problem

Too many computer users have learned only one way to solve a problem—they turn off the computer. On a network, this "solution" is disastrous if the user is using a server as a workstation. Since the server also has open files for other users, everyone may be affected by this rash solution. It is important to recover from the mistake, not ignore it.

Develop and publish a list of steps when problems are encountered on the network. Those steps might include the following.

1. Read the screen for indications of the next step or keypress.
2. Press the [F1] key for help.
3. Read the manual for the software. (With LAN software, this may require the arduous task of locating the manual first.)
4. Ask others who may have had the problem before.
5. Call or locate the support person (probably the system administrator).
6. If a reboot or power down is required on a server, warn the other users and allow them to exit from their programs on the server first.

Report the Problem

Regardless of the recovery or restart, the problem should be noted somewhere. An E-mail or paper note to the administrator is very helpful. Because LAN problems can be intermittent, these reports may provide a pattern the administrator can notice when the information comes from several sources.

The report can be very minimal. It should include the user's name, the date, and the time of the incident. The user should explain what happened prior to the problem, what the problem looked like, and how the problem was resolved. While one or more of these elements may be missing, anything provided by the user can be helpful. A sample report might look like this:

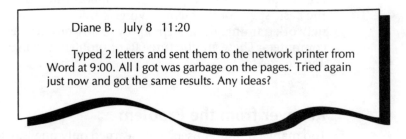

Diane B. July 8 11:20

Typed 2 letters and sent them to the network printer from Word at 9:00. All I got was garbage on the pages. Tried again just now and got the same results. Any ideas?

Re-create the Problem

The best approach to solving problems once and for all is to re-create them. In the example, Diane thought the problem might be related to the network, so she waited for a few hours and tried again, with the same results. In this case, the problem is more likely to be the printer setting within Word, possibly still set for Diane's local laser printer. By re-creating a problem, you can learn to avoid those circumstances in the future or at least be prepared for the problem when it occurs.

Checklist

Before sitting down to begin the installation, make sure you have

_____ Read enough of the manuals to understand the installation steps and additional information provided.

_____ Left enough time to install, troubleshoot, and test the installation.

_____ Gathered enough floppy disks to make backup copies of all the programs.

_____ Completed your network plan, including a list of users.

Once you have finished the installation, you need to make sure you have

_____ Documented the resources on the server, including all LAN programs.

_____ Scheduled training for the users.

_____ Filled out and mailed all the warranty cards.

_____ Provided the users with a contact for technical support.

7

Summary

When you are setting up your first network, the software installation should be a bit less intimidating than the hardware installation. If you have a good idea of the basics and have planned as much as possible, yes. As long as you get over any aversion to manuals, take your time, and rely on your list of technical support names, you can do it.

This chapter also discussed

+ The usefulness of setting up a two-system test location.

+ The need to install the server first, without trying to work out all the details on the first installation.

+ The need to be prepared for different installation parameters on different workstations.

+ The minimum daily requirement to test, test, and test some more.

+ The critical need to provide structured training for users, both before and after the network is installed.

CHAPTER

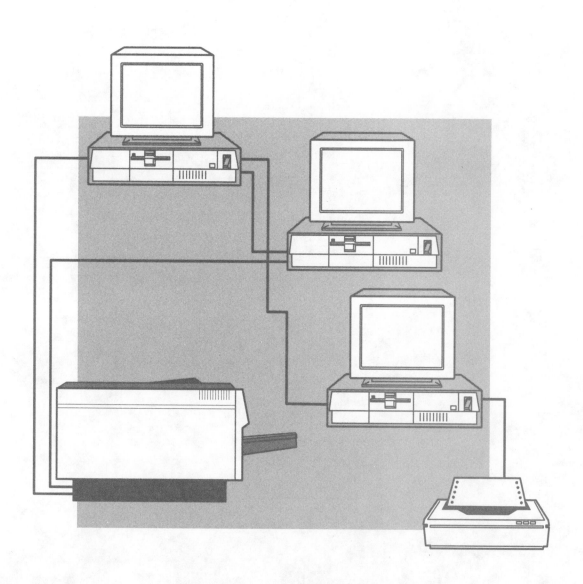

NETWORK MAINTENANCE

Keeping the network running smoothly requires constant effort. The more stations and software running on the network, the more areas you'll need to watch for problems. This chapter provides an outline of network maintenance tasks, such as backing up data, disaster preparation, and hard disk maintenance. User training and technical support are also emphasized in the chapter. This chapter's checklist helps you determine daily, weekly, and monthly network maintenance schedules.

This chapter covers a wide range of maintenance issues. You'll discover that networked printers need additional attention from both the users and the administrator. As network supervisor, you'll manage the user list, directory resources, and the massive number of files that accumulate on the server. You may also want to improve performance on the network. And you'll definitely want users to continue to learn and benefit from the network.

Even before you begin thinking about network maintenance, you may want to consider the attitude of the users attached to the LAN. These users may perceive themselves as part of a group and share the responsibilities of managing a network, or they may see themselves only as users, served by "someone else." Your approach to network maintenance should be as carefully planned as the installation. You need to determine which of these two approaches you want the network users to take. Do you want them to become dependent upon you or to accomplish as much as they can on their own?

You'll need to decide who will be responsible for the daily and extended maintenance on the network. Someone needs to keep printers supplied with paper. Someone needs to create and delete users and user file access. Someone needs to manage the server files. And someone needs to provide general support for the inevitable network and application problems.

As you read this chapter, assess the skill level required to perform these tasks. Then, depending on how you want to structure the network support system, determine who might be able to perform them. The worksheet at the end of the chapter will then help you create a maintenance checklist for the network.

Managing Printers

Depending on the network software, users have the potential to send data to any printer on the network. While this may provide a greater variety of printers for each user, it also requires more management of each printer. The user closest to the printer must understand how his or her system functions as a printer server. For printers attached to a dedicated server, printout delivery is a concern. But before you can manage the printer, you need to know about the print spooler software.

Using the Network Printer

All network users need to understand how printer data is handled on the network. The network programs include a *print spooler,* which allows the network to accept multiple inputs from different users at the same time for the same printer. The program saves each user's printer data to disk. As the printer completes one job, the spooler software looks for the next job on the disk and begins sending that document to the network printer.

An additional advantage of simultaneous printer input from users is the control of the data being sent to the printer. Each document sent to the network printer becomes a *print job.* These jobs can be tracked, deleted, or reprioritized with a network program. For example, NetWare Lite uses a program called PRINT. LANtastic users manage printer jobs from the main menu under Printer Queue Management. Once this option is selected, the screen shown in Figure 8-1 appears.

Access to the print queue may vary with different networks. Some allow only the supervisor to make any changes, while others allow users to modify what they have sent to the network printer. The changes include putting a print job on hold, deleting a print job, restarting a print job, and changing the order of the print queue. This flexibility

8

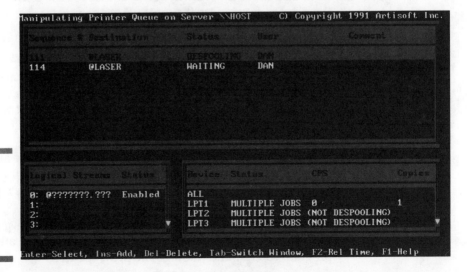

The printer queue management screen from LANtastic
Figure 8-1.

allows larger jobs to be scheduled to print later in the day or in the evening. It also requires someone with access to the queue to manage the print job list.

TIP: To practice using the print spooler program, leave the network printer off. Send several documents as you normally would to the network printer. Then use the network software to delete or make other changes to the list of print jobs on the screen.

The User's Printer Responsibilities

Anyone using a workstation with a network printer attached must be aware of the additional responsibilities and limitations that come with that station. While the responsibilities may be shared between the user and the administrator, the limitations relate to the dual use of the computer: The user is running applications while the network is routing print jobs to the printer. The limitations may affect the user in the following ways, depending on the network software:

✦ Because the server software requires memory, less memory is available to run applications on the system.

✦ Hard disk space must always be available for the network to store the printer data before it spools off to the printer.

✦ The application program, such as word processing, may slow down while the network handles the print job.

✦ You may not always get to use "your" printer immediately. If someone else starts a 50-page print job, you can send your document to the network print spool, but the output won't appear until the other user's 50 pages have been printed.

The responsibilities of the user with a network printer are also important. These also apply to a dedicated server with a printer attached:

✦ Never turn off or reboot the computer unless you are sure the network printer spooler is empty. Network programs all provide a program to view and manage the print spooler.

+ Make sure other users have access to the printer room; don't lock the door every time you leave.

+ Keep a specific type of paper in the printer. For example, with a wide 130-column dot matrix printer, users might assume it has 14-inch-wide paper. Users need to know if the paper is changed.

+ Keep the printer loaded with a good supply of paper, enough to last at least a day, unattended. If the user/administrator must be gone longer than that, make sure someone watches the paper supply.

+ Always make sure the on-line light is lit. If it is off, the network spooler will accept and store print jobs, but it won't be able to send them to the printer. When someone finally does switch the printer back on, the printer may run for hours.

+ Watch the ribbon or toner. If the image is too light, change the ribbon or toner or notify someone that it needs to be changed.

Loading Paper into the Printer

Some users are timid about changing paper in the printer. Even with the newer tractor-feed printers, users still need to know how to operate the automatic loading feature. Laser printer paper trays also have quirks users need to be aware of.

Any training session should include loading paper into printers, as well as how to use the on-line switch. Allow each participant to load and unload the printer several times. This is probably the most physical thing they will do with their computer systems. The repetition will help them remember all the steps.

Delivering Printer Output

Because network printers are shared, the hard copy is generated from many different users. The user may be next to the printer and able to retrieve the material immediately. Other users may be down the hall or farther away. Walking this distance from workstation to printer may prove to be a great waste of time.

Some users will send the job to the printer and immediately get up to retrieve the output. This might include a stroll down the hall, a chance to chat with a few people along the way, and then having to wait at the printer for several other jobs already in the queue.

As the system administrator, and possibly the boss, you'll have to decide if those repetitive trips are worth the time. Chapter 2 suggested taking a close look at the use of both local and network printers. If you are leaning toward fewer, but networked, printers, you may want to consider ways to minimize this lost time. One alternative is to offer delivery of the hard copy. If this service is provided on a schedule, possibly every hour, the users don't need to make the trip, and they'll know when to expect their printouts.

This alternative to the "printer stroll" has additional advantages:

+ The material is kept more confidential; users aren't reading through the stack of pages to find their printouts.

+ The server, with attached printers, can be kept more secure, with access limited to the network administrator and the printer manager.

+ The paper and ribbon or toner replacement is the responsibility of just one person, the printer manager.

There are several disadvantages to such strict printer control:

+ Users must wait for their hard copy until the next delivery.

+ This method of printout routing is a return to the centralized computing model from the mainframe days.

+ Someone must add the job of "network printer manager" to his or her responsibilities.

Whatever method you choose to manage the printers, this is one area where daily attention will be required.

Managing Users, Files, and Directories

The network represents a dynamic resource. Users' needs for file space, programs, and directory access may change frequently. The original network plan that showed the directory tree and resources on the server needs to be constantly updated. As the network administrator, you'll need to add and change users as well as change user and group access to files on the server.

Managing User Accounts

The small network of six or eight users does not require much account maintenance. The supervisor must establish the users' accounts when the network is first installed. Once the users successfully log on for the first time, the supervisor may have little to do. The only changes might be to delete a former employee and add the new one. Users may be able to make some modifications to their own accounts, such as changing their passwords or temporarily disabling their accounts.

When first setting up these accounts, you have a number of variables to provide. On a small network, you may elect to skip some of these choices or just accept the default settings. Here are a few of the items you can select for network users:

◆ **The user's account name** The user's account name is typically the user's first name. If you have more than one user with the same first name, you can make the names unique by adding the first letter of the last name—for example, JOHNJ and JOHNH. Or you might use the first initial of the first and middle names and then as much of the last name as possible— for example, DRBOID for Dennis Raymond Boid.

◆ **A description of the user** The description can be the user's full name, department, or job title. Use whatever helps you identify the users beyond their account names.

◆ **Password requirements** A password is always recommended on even a small network. In addition to having the user respond Y/N to a password requirement, you may be able to set an expiration date so that the user must change the password at regular intervals.

◆ **User privileges** The user privileges choice sets the level of access the user has to the network. For example, NetWare Lite allows user access at the supervisor level. With that access, the user can see and use everyone's files and make significant, and potentially disastrous, changes to the network.

8

With most systems, you need only create the user name, and an account is active. Some networks start with a general access level, and have you either restrict or expand the level. Others require that you specify exactly what the user can access. Without that information in the user's account, the user will be able to log on the network but will not be able to do anything else.

Changing Directory Resources

The directories originally available on the network are based on your first plan. You may quickly discover that you did not provide enough directories or that groups of users need new directories to share group-related files.

Several problems may occur as you make changes to the directory structure on the server. The most common is just keeping track of what is available on the server and who has access. You can reduce this confusion if you keep an up-to-date map of all these resources. If your users are actively involved in this design, they should be provided with a copy of this map. The map could even be kept as a file in a public directory. Anyone who wants to view the current settings could access the file.

This level of openness may not be desirable if different users have access to different areas. You may need to create a list of users with specific access areas on the server's hard disk. If your users rely on a menu to access server programs and files, you may spend a lot of time changing these individual menus unless you have created a common network menu.

Another problem with changing directories relates to the user's drive access letter. Remember that you only create the resource and name it. The actual drive letter on the workstation can potentially be different for every user, depending on that user's logon script or batch file. Although users may be sharing the same files, one user may talk about getting the files off M while another user has that resource as drive O. This is difficult to track for everyone.

You may want to create a general plan for network drives. Assuming your first network drive starts at F, you have 21 drives to use, F through Z. You could determine that all users access the C:\MAIL\CCMAIL subdirectory as drive M. Access to the network utilities might be from drive U. Making these resources and drive designations consistent across the network and keeping a record of the changes will save everyone time in the long run.

Protecting Common Files

As you first set up the server and open new subdirectories, remember to protect the commonly used files in that area. This may mean limiting access to those files by making the directory read-only or by making individual files read-only with the DOS ATTRIB command. (See the DOS manual for more information about the syntax of the ATTRIB command.) This prevents accidental deletion by users or, worse yet, a user replacing one version of the program with another.

Managing Server Data

The files stored on the server are like all the neighborhood's gardening tools being kept in a single garage. Keeping the tools organized and limiting access helps prevent problems for a while, but eventually the garage will fill up. Likewise, users may just keep shoving in files without looking to see how full the server is.

Your job as supervisor will be not only to organize the files into directories, but also to determine the space available and work with the users to periodically clean out their subdirectories. Some network programs even allow you to limit the amount of space available to users. Once you have addressed the housekeeping issue, you also must consider the possibility of viruses on the network.

Housekeeping

At the first level, housekeeping is the user's responsibility. You can emphasize this by letting the users know that the server is not a limitless resource, capable of storing all the files the users want to create. You may want to offer the following suggestions for file maintenance:

✦ Develop a naming convention for files. For example, if a file is temporary, automatically start the filename with a "T." Then, when you are cleaning out the directory, you can easily delete all files beginning with a "T" by using DEL T*.*.

◆ Set aside a specific time for housekeeping. Friday afternoon might a good choice.

◆ If in doubt about a file's value, copy the file to a floppy disk before erasing it from the network.

◆ Check the date stamps on files to determine which files to examine first. MS-DOS 5.0 and many utility programs allow you to view a directory sorted by date. You can then work from the top of the directory list with the oldest files.

◆ Print the directory to the printer with the DIR > LPT1 command. Check off or cross out files as each is examined.

◆ Consider a utility that works with network drives and allows files to be marked and deleted in one step.

◆ You can also use file compression programs such as PKZIP to save space for infrequently used files that need to remain accessible on the server.

As the administrator, your responsibility is to watch the remaining space on the server hard drive. If you keep a daily or weekly log of the space available, you may be able to project when the hard disk will fill up. You have several options when a full hard disk appears imminent. You can

◆ Buy and install another hard disk.

◆ Encourage users to do some serious housekeeping.

◆ Begin limiting hard disk space by user account.

◆ Reconsider your network design and use of hard disk space on the server.

You need to let your users know what might happen when the hard disk fills up. Potentially, a user could lose a document, the print spooler could quit working or the network might crash completely for lack of temporary file space.

Coping with Computer Viruses

If you don't know much about computer viruses, this is the time to learn about them—the easy way. A LAN increases the possibility of exposure because of the number of users on the network. Fortunately, antivirus programs exist to combat the problem. The best approach is to be prepared for possible viruses before they infect your system. The rest of this section provides more information about viruses and then focuses on how to prevent them.

Computer viruses are programs intentionally written to disrupt system usage. Results of a virus may range from a message displayed at random on the screen to total deletion of data on a hard or floppy disk. There are several types of viruses, and some systems are more likely to encounter a virus than others. Unfortunately, viruses have become prevalent enough that routine system maintenance should include running a special virus detection and repair program.

Types of Viruses

The term "computer virus" also includes other programs intended to disrupt a computer system or an entire network. A *Trojan horse* is a program that appears to do one thing while actually doing something else. For example, you run a program called SMILE. A smiley face appears on the screen and disappears 30 seconds later. What you don't know is that the program was erasing your hard disk while the image appeared on the screen. This program is not a true virus because it destroys itself in the process of creating the damage. This is small consolation, however, for the user just discovering the massive amount of lost data.

A *worm* is the type of virus commonly found on networks. This type of program uses the connections between computers to transmit itself. In the process of searching for systems, it takes up system resources and may cause a network-wide shutdown.

The virus *bomb* is a program that runs every time the system is booted. The bomb checks the system date. At a predetermined date such as Friday the 13th, the program activates and damages the system or just announces its presence. This program may also attempt to spread itself through networks and on floppy disks. The Michelangelo virus is a well-known virus bomb. On March 6, Michelangelo's birthday, the

8

virus erases nine megabytes of hard disk space. At all other times, it just tries to duplicate itself onto other systems.

How Viruses Spread

Virus programs, like diseases, are spread through contact with virus-infected systems. A virus can infect your system in one of several ways. The most common way occurs when you accept a floppy from someone and run a program from that floppy on your system. If that program contains a virus, the virus will copy itself to your system and begin doing damage. If you copy that same program to a floppy and give it to someone else, that person's system will then be infected.

Sharing programs of unknown origin increases the risk of spreading a virus. Exchanging data files on disk is not likely to spread a virus. A virus can be spread only when a program containing the virus is run. A spreadsheet or database data file from a floppy or network drive is not likely to carry a virus.

In addition to being transferred from disks, virus-containing programs can be downloaded from bulletin board systems. Thousands of files are available on BBSs and can be easily exchanged. One user can send the file to the BBS and within days, dozens of callers can copy that file to their systems, run the program, and be infected by the virus. Many BBS system operators (SYSOPs) now certify that their files are virus free by running virus-detection programs on the files before releasing them to be copied by other callers.

Virus transmission is also very possible over a network. The more user access to the network, the higher the probability that a virus will invade the system. As noted with the worm virus, some of these programs are designed to seek out and transmit themselves over networks. It is possible for a virus to attach itself to the network software and infect all users attached to the server.

What are the chances a virus can infect a network? The following list suggests minimum to maximum virus risk levels. The highest risk level applies to only one user because that one user can infect everyone else on the network.

✦ **Very unlikely** Everyone on the network runs only commercial programs and copies data files to floppy disks only for backup.

+ **Possible** Some users have public-domain programs, and files are copied both to and from other systems through the network or with floppy disks.

+ **Very likely** Most users use a mix of public domain, shareware, and commercial programs. Users frequently pass programs around by copying the files to the server.

+ **Highly likely** Program files are frequently copied from BBSs and commercial services and run without being checked for viruses.

As in many situations with the computer, prevention and detection are the best ways to remain virus free. Educating your network users is the first major step. These precautions and regular use of an antivirus program significantly reduce your risk of virus infection and data loss:

+ Never use a program of unknown origin.

+ Never copy programs to the hard disk without knowing the source of the program. The more useless the program appears, the better chance it has a virus attached.

+ Be careful when copying files from a floppy to the hard disk with the COPY *.* command. An unwanted file can be copied along with the data files you expect. Use COPY with specific filenames to make sure you get only what you expect in the transaction.

+ Use a hard disk protection program to prevent unexpected access to the disk. These programs may totally prevent hard disk access or provide a warning when a program writes to the disk. You would use this only when running a program of unknown origin; otherwise, you won't be able to save files on the hard disk.

+ Run CHKDSK every week or so if your network software allows it. (NetWare doesn't.) If CHKDSK gives "Lost cluster" messages regularly, a virus may be eating parts of files.

TIP: If possible, reserve one system not connected to the network to try all new, untested software. Run the software for at least several days and check it with a virus-detection program prior to general distribution or use on the network.

Virus Detection and Cure

One example of a virus protection program is Central Point Anti-Virus (CPAV), a Central Point Software product. Even before installing itself on a local or network hard disk, the software checks for over 1000 viruses. If it finds any, it removes them before going any further in the installation.

Once installed, CPAV automatically checks memory when the system is booted up and then "watches" in the background for viruses attempting entry into your system. If the workstations cannot afford to use 40K of memory to run an antivirus TSR, users can execute an antivirus program to periodically check memory and the hard disk for any viruses. You can use the program on the network at any time to check for viruses.

By their nature, viruses continue to evolve. Most antivirus program vendors operate a 24-hour hotline, provide quarterly mailings, and have forums with on-line services for downloading new antivirus update files. When looking for an antivirus program, make sure you can easily access the updated files for your network.

Because some virus programs are designed to cause only occasional problems, the pattern of damage may be hard to detect. Possible symptoms include frequent lost clusters, bad or unreadable parts of files, and slow disk access times. The network system administrator should perform a virus check as part of routine maintenance. Figure 8-2 shows the results of a virus scan by Central Point Anti-Virus.

Protecting the Server Files

One of your reasons for installing a LAN may have been to provide better data backup. The users were not backing up their data on their local hard drives, so you designed the network for data file storage on the server. Now that you have all the company's eggs in one basket, you must be absolutely sure that data is backed up on a regular basis.

Part of your network plan should include a regular backup system. Originally, you may have decided that a stack of disks and an hour a week were all you needed. If you have changed your mind and would rather not spend all that time, you may want to purchase additional

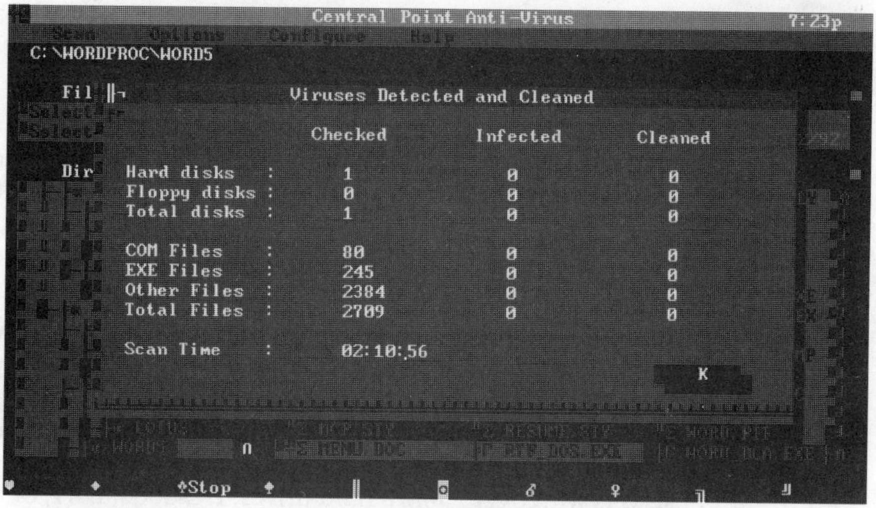

The results of a virus scan by Central Point Anti-Virus
Figure 8-2.

equipment to make that process easier. If you want the equipment but can't afford it yet, don't stop doing the floppy disk backups.

Tape drives are the most popular and least expensive alternative to backing up data on disk. But in between the backup sessions, you are still very vulnerable to data loss from power outages. You may also need to consider an uninterruptable power supply.

Using Tape Drives for Backups

A minicartridge tape drive backup system saves both time and effort for a small network administrator. Because the tape capacities start at 20MB, the entire contents of a small hard disk can be copied to one tape. You need not sit next to the computer and insert floppy disks every minute as the system backs up. In fact, many backup programs allow you to perform an unattended backup. You leave the tape in the drive and set the backup program to execute at a specific time, typically late at night.

Moderate capacity, 60- to 250MB tape drives are available as both internal and external units and can cost as little as $200. The internal devices fit in one drive bay. Most small networks have the tape drive in the server. Internal and external drives conforming to the QIC-80 standard format use the same tape cartridges to save the files. The total time for backing up will vary with the tape drive system and the amount of data to be saved. For a 120MB backup, the total time should be less than an hour.

Some backup programs allow the tape drive to also back up the hard disk in each workstation. This too is usually an unattended operation. The user leaves on the workstation overnight with the backup program set for a specific time. Once the time is reached, the backup program copies all the designated files from the workstation to the tape backup unit in the server.

You should consider purchasing a minicartridge tape drive system if backups are being performed erratically or if someone must spend more than half an hour when backing up the server every day. If you want to perform an unattended backup, you'll have to use a drive with at least as much capacity as the hard drive space on the server. For larger servers with over 250MB hard drives, DC-8000, DAT, or 8mm tape drives are better alternatives.

TIP: When considering a tape drive unit, include the cost of at least seven to ten tape cartridges in the original purchase and, depending on your archive needs, additional tapes to save backed up files permanently.

Remember the basic rules for backing up, whether with disks or tapes: Always rotate the disks or tapes, and keep the most recent backups in a different location.

Rotation of the disks or tapes means that you have more than one copy of the files. In most cases you should have at least three generations of backups for each of the types of backups performed. For example, you may do a complete backup every weekend and perform an incremental backup daily. You would have three tapes for the last three full backups and you might have a tape for each day of the week. If you lose a complete drive on Thursday, you can restore the system from the last full backup and then restore each of the previous days, Monday through Wednesday. If the most recent weekly tape had errors, you could use the next most recent tape.

Always keep a set of backups in some other location. This anticipates a total disaster in which the company office is destroyed. A good approach is for the system administrator to take the most recent tape home every evening and return with the third most recent tape, leaving the second most recent at home. This means that a set of backups is still at home during the day and two sets are at home during the night.

Preventing File Loss with a UPS

When a computer unexpectedly loses power, the operating system is unable to properly close data files in use. On a desktop computer, this may mean the user loses some data from one or more files. For a server, with dozens of files open at one time, this power loss may be a disaster for everyone on the network. To prevent this potential disaster, you can connect the server to an uninterruptable power supply (UPS).

A UPS provides a steady stream of electrical power for periods of time ranging from ten minutes to several hours when normal power is disrupted. The reserve power depends on the size of the UPS and the number of devices attached to it. In most cases, the UPS is plugged into the wall and the devices are then plugged into the UPS. Some UPS devices can be installed inside the computer. When power is lost, the UPS instantly switches to internal batteries and continues to provide power. When this power loss is very short, the attached devices never notice the change. If the power loss is longer, the UPS provides power until the batteries are exhausted.

8

With a UPS connected to the server, a brief power loss or fluctuation allows the network to continue functioning without rebooting and losing files. Of course, the users' systems may automatically reboot in the process unless they also have a UPS.

Some UPS units include a cable to connect to a serial port on the server. When power has been lost for a preset length of time, such as ten minutes, the UPS signals the network to shut down. The network closes all open files and warns users that the network server is shutting down. (On a small network, the users may not see the message since their systems are already off at that point.)

Any location that experiences frequent power brownouts or fluctuations may require a UPS to protect the server. Less expensive units, under $300, are rated at 500 watts for ten minutes. These are primarily intended to provide protection from power shifts. Larger and more expensive units provide the connection with the server and offer protection for longer delays. You should assess the potential damage to your data and work flow to determine the need for or level of a UPS attached to your network server.

TIP: Many network consultants consider a UPS a critical component in a NetWare network. Experience has shown that with NetWare networks, power failures invariably result in lost or damaged data files.

Network Performance

Once the network is installed and running fairly smoothly, you may be interested in improving performance. From the user's point of view, this means faster access to the server and less waiting for hard copy from the networked printers. It may also mean less downtime when the network fails and a quicker response from support people. Improving one or more of these areas enhances everyone's use of and satisfaction with the network.

As with any changes to a computer system, make the changes carefully and be certain you can undo any modifications you make. With hardware, this approach means that you keep the old equipment until you are sure the new equipment is what you really want. With software, you make a complete set of backups just before you modify any files; if the change does not work, you need to be able to restore the files.

As with any modifications on an existing network, do the work when users are not likely to need access. Sundays starting at 7:00 A.M. are a good time. No one is likely to be in the office then. And you have 24 hours before someone comes in to use the network, enough time to either make the change successfully or to recover from the mistakes.

Redistributing the Printer Load

The network printer may prove to be a bottleneck for users. If they have to wait a long time to get their hard copy, you may have lost any advantages you had by purchasing one fast printer instead of several slower printers. As discussed in Chapter 2, you may need to reconsider where the printers are located.

The quickest way to evaluate printer performance is to ask the users:

✦ Are they waiting too long for the network output? (While "too long" is subjective, the phrase still conveys a sense of tolerance for the delays.)

✦ Is the improved quality worth the wait?

✦ Is someone using the printer so much that print jobs are delayed?

✦ Are they printing more or less now that they are using the network printer?

✦ Is their workload increased or decreased now that they are using the network printer?

✦ Do they spend too much time retrieving their hard copy from the network printer?

The distribution of printers on a small network may be a trial-and-error effort. Only after the network has been installed and used can people begin to answer those types of questions.

8

Most laser printers include counters. You can record these every month by looking "under the hood" and noting the count. After a few months, you'll know where the heavy printing is being done.

TIP: Watching the counter is also a good way to lengthen the life of several printers. Rotate the heavy and light load printers among the users.

If you have a mixture of network and local printers without counters, you can assess use by monitoring the paper supply. Ask users to note the date, the amount of paper, and their names when they grab paper for their printer. If you have a more formal supply system, you can just use the requisitions. After a few months of gathering paper-use records, you can determine who is using their printers the most. Those using the least paper may be served adequately by the network printer. Their printers can then be provided to those who complain the most about having to use the network printer.

Another way to improve printer service is to purchase a faster printer. If the printer is running constantly, you may want to upgrade to a heavy-duty printer. There are several printers now rated for the higher speed and heavy-duty cycle of a network. Many of the current printers used as network printers were designed only as personal printers. Heavy use just wears them out more quickly.

Another way to increase printed copy production is to purchase a second printer for the server. If the laser printer is being used to capacity, install a less expensive dot matrix printer and request that all but final drafts be sent to the second, dot matrix printer. This distribution of the load might ease the strain on the laser and prolong its operation.

Improving Response Times

Network users should understand that delays might occur when they use a network drive to access files. Depending on a number of factors, this delay may not be much more than when they access a local drive, or the delay may last many seconds. If the delays are too long, users will avoid using the network or complain loudly when they do. As system administrator, you have several ways to improve this performance.

Remember, however, to make only one change at a time. This way you can test the result and more easily return to the previous setup if necessary.

Locating Potential Network Faults

If you notice a change in the performance of the network, you may have a network software or hardware problem. This may occur if connectors come loose, network cards begin to fail, or for any of dozens of other reasons. This is when the problem logs kept by the users may help track down the cause. If the logs show a specific date and time when everyone noted a problem, you may be able to determine what changed on that day.

TIP: A problem log is a list maintained by users. They use it when they notice specific problems or unusual occurrences on the network. In the log, users should make a note including the date, the time, and specifically what they were doing when they noticed the problem. E-mail is a good way to funnel these logs to the network administrator.

There are a number of network utility programs that watch network traffic and can sometimes pinpoint cable and card faults. While not cheap, the software may save days of searching for the problems. You may also want to consider using a consultant when you encounter new problems on a network that had, until that point, been functioning fine.

If the network is functioning normally but you want to improve its performance, you can fine-tune the network software, reorganize the network, or purchase faster hardware.

Using a Disk Cache

Most network server programs include disk cache (pronounced "cash") settings. A *disk cache* stores data in memory as well as on the hard disk. Because memory can be accessed more quickly than hard disks, the software first looks in memory for the data requested. If the cache program finds the data in memory, it responds to the request more quickly than if it must read the data from the hard disk. The larger the amount of memory devoted to the cache, the more data can be stored temporarily, and the more frequently the cache can find and send the data from memory.

To improve performance with the disk cache, you increase the amount of memory allocated to the cache. Either you can physically add more memory to the server or, depending on the network software, you may be able to leave less for the application programs to run. If yours is a dedicated system, you may need to leave only a small amount of memory and use the rest for cache. Your network manuals provide more information about the network cache program, or, depending on the software, you may be able to use third-party disk cache programs.

Speeding Up Disk Access

As files are opened, closed, and deleted, the physical spaces used by those files may no longer be continuous. When the file segments are no longer connected on the disk, the disk has become *fragmented.* On the server, this fragmentation occurs fairly quickly. When files are fragmented, the hard drive must work harder to locate and read the discontinuous parts of each file. The disk head must jump from one part of the file to the next. This slows access times for those files, delaying access time for everyone using the server's hard disk as a resource.

Utility programs such as Central Point's PC Tools 7.1 provide a defragmentation program, sometimes also called a compression or disk optimization program. This type of program examines the hard disk for files physically located in different parts of the disk and reports the percentage of fragmentation. Most of these programs recommend that you run them when the disk has more than 2 percent fragmentation. While running, the program moves file segments around to place all the segments together, one after the other. The result is no empty holes in the hard disk file structure.

You must, however, check your network manuals. Some, such as NOVELL NetWare 2.2, cannot be optimized by third-party programs because the drive does not use a standard DOS format. The drive optimization program will also tell you if it will not work on a network drive.

Because a defragmentation program works with the hard disk very intensely, you'll need to run the program during off-hours. In many cases, the programs require a reboot of the server because the file tables in memory no longer match the file tables as arranged by the optimization program. For this reason, you should run the program from the server instead of a workstation.

The frequency with which you run this program will depend on the percentage of fragmentation you see in a week's or month's time. When combined with a disk cache program, regular optimization improves the performance of your server.

Focusing Processor Power

If the network access speed is still not acceptable after you have maximized the cache and optimized the disk, you may need to make the system a dedicated server. With peer-to-peer software such as LANtastic, you can increase performance by inserting a program command line in the startup batch file called ALONE. This allows the network software to concentrate on just handling network requests and not on having to check for local user requests as well.

With a program such as NetWare 2.2, you must install the software for either a nondedicated or dedicated server. Making the switch from nondedicated to dedicated may take longer and require a complete reinstallation. In both cases, the result should be improved performance. The processor does not have to flip back and forth between the local tasks and the network tasks.

Upgrading Hardware

You can also increase network speed by upgrading your hardware. You can replace the hard disk with one that has faster access times. You can also replace the processor with the next generation. You might even discover that you are using an 8-bit network card in the server when it could hold a 16-bit. For example, upgrading the server card from an 8- to a 16-bit card with NetWare results in a signficant increase in performance. As with all changes, take these one at a time.

Hardware improvements are likely to require outside help from a consultant. You'll need to balance the consultant's recommendations and costs against the anticipated performance increase. You should get this expected improvement in writing from the consultant before the work begins.

8

Disk access speed is a good place to start. Even a good disk cache program cannot make up for a very slow hard drive. Utility programs can report the average seek time of a hard disk. If the drive has average seek times of over 20 milliseconds, the drive is not likely to provide good performance on a server. You may want to consider getting a new drive with faster access. You might consider getting a larger hard drive as well.

Even if the drive is fast enough, the processor may not be. You may replace the server motherboard with one using a faster processor. For example, you might move from a 286 to a 386 to improve response times. Depending on many other variables, you may be able to use many of the old components such as the floppy drives and display card.

As with any major project, this may take several days and include reinstalling the network software.

You may need to consider upgrading the network protocol you are using. For example, if you originally selected ARCnet cards because they were less expensive, you may need to replace them with Ethernet cards and cable to get the performance you need. Making a change at this level requires a major overhaul of the network and is recommended only if network performance cannot be improved by any other methods.

Planning Crash Procedures

Just as you prepare for fires by having a fire drill, you need to plan ahead for server crashes. When the server stops running for any reason, the severity of the problem depends on the network design. If everyone depends on the server for all files, everyone's work grinds to a halt. If, on the other hand, users just access the server for printers and E-mail, the crash will not be as disruptive.

In all cases, you need to have established a series of steps to let users know whom to contact, what to expect, and how to deal with the worst-case situation.

When the server stops working on a small network, the users know whom to call—you. But if you are not in the office, you need to have established a list of steps to deal with the problem. This may mean someone else in the office takes over. Or it may mean you call your local consultant immediately. This list of people should include names and phone numbers and be readily available (it can be taped to the side of the server).

In the first few minutes after the crash, users are left wondering what happened and how long it will take before the server is restored. In those same first few minutes, you are trying to determine what caused the problem. While you are engrossed in solving the problem, users may be sitting quietly, not doing anything, expecting the system to recover soon.

As soon as you have any indication of the problem and the length of time it will take to solve, let the users know. Use the public address system or just have someone trot down the hall making the announcement. Give the users an idea of how long the system may be down. If you don't know what happened or how long it will take, let them know that. At least they can begin working on something different until they can return to using the network. Part of your network orientation sessions should also include this information about what to do and what to expect when the server quits working.

Once the server is back up, you need to let users know they can·log on again. Depending on the network, this may mean running a startup batch file or performing a simple log on command. Make sure this has been spelled out in the documentation you've provided.

If you know the server will not be back up in any reasonable length of time (say, for more than a day), you need to have a backup system. This can be a system from the local retailer or consultant or another system on the network. At a minimum, you'll need to transfer the backed-up files to the new server. If you use a tape drive backup, you may need to move the drive to that second system to restore the latest version of the files. Or you may be able to move the server's hard drive to the second system, depending on the cause of the server crash in the first place.

The real key to surviving a server crash is to be prepared. Remember, it is not "if" the server will crash, but "when."

User Support

While caught up in the maintenance of the hardware and software, don't forget the network users. They need to be kept informed of all pending changes on the network. They should be asked what they need to make their use of the network easier. This ease of use includes knowing where to turn for help and continuing to learn more about their computers.

Establishing a Support Team

With a small network, you are likely to be the office "guru," especially if you installed the network yourself. The users look to you for answers and help for all their network and computer problems. Because you will not always be available, you need to design a support team. You may be the team leader, but when you can teach others how to solve the problems everyone encounters, you take the pressure off yourself and you provide the users with more support resources.

Just as you plan for a server crash, anticipate your absence and prepare for it. Let all the users know who is on the team and who is the second in command. A well-structured team also includes specialists. In a small office with a small network, this may mean that everyone has an area of specialization. If you realize there are software programs no one knows much about, you may want to develop a continuing education plan for your whole support team (everyone in the office).

Encouraging Continued Learning

There are a lot of ways to learn about computers. While some people may be able and willing to learn by trial and error, other users prefer more structure. If you provide the incentive and example, you and the network users may be interested in using one or more of the following methods to learn more about computers and software productivity.

Take Classes

Colleges provide evening classes related to the use of computers. If you need a structured setting to learn about computers, these classes can improve your skills. Following are several things to do before signing up for a class.

Decide what you want to get out of the computer course. If you want to learn how to use Word for Windows, have two or more examples of the documents you might create at work. If you just want to know what Word for Windows is, you may get all you need to know in the first class and waste a semester learning more than you really wanted.

Talk with people who have taken the class. Find out if their goals were met and how well structured the class was. Ask what they thought of the instructor and the equipment. Did they have lots of lab nights when there was no instruction? Did they really need that time to work on the class assignments? Did the instructor provide help during those labs?

Call the instructor. Ask the instructor how long he or she has used the software being taught in the class. Ask for a specific description of the instructor's last project using the software.

Call the department head about the lab equipment. Ask about the type of computer and version of software used in the course. You'll want to compare that with the equipment and software you use at the office or have at home. If the school's version of the software is older, you may be frustrated by the limitations of the older software imposed in class. If your equipment is older or you are using an older version of the software, you can determine if you want to improve your system or upgrade your software. You may also learn a few features in class not available back at work.

Find out when you can drop the class and still get a refund. If you attend the first class and don't feel that the course will do much for you, at least you'll know you can still get a partial or full refund.

After the course has begun in earnest, remember that the more you put into the course, the more you will learn. You are taking the class to learn how to use the computer, not just to get a grade. If the instructor does not know the answer, ask for someone who does. If the equipment fails, make sure you get compensation time. Attend class even if it is scheduled as "open lab" and you can do the work on a computer elsewhere. The instructor may provide some nuggets of information you would not otherwise hear. Insist that the class be conducted the full scheduled time. The point of taking the class is access to the resources. Allowing the instructor to dismiss class an hour early wastes your tuition money and time.

Get Training

The term "training" is typically used to describe shorter, noncredit courses provided in the business environment. Chapter 7 offered some suggestions for the training provided to introduce users to the network. You may want to continue providing regular training on the network and other computer-related topics.

The most effective training courses are designed specifically for your company or department, using examples from your daily work. Attendees have probably worked with the software or at least have seen what other people in the company have done with it. Lecture and computer time should be in a ratio of about one to two. An hour spent explaining the concepts and providing examples can then lead to two hours of hands-on computer time.

Many software and hardware vendors provide or recommend training sites and instructors. Some "certifications" are more substantial than others. Contact the vendor to determine the actual relationship for any training company claiming a connection with a software or hardware manufacturer.

Join User Groups

Any semiregular gathering of computer users can be designated as a user group. The purpose is for members to help each other learn more about computers and software. Some user groups are organized around specific computers; others are based on software packages. Six people may casually meet every week in a restaurant, or the group may be large enough to be more formal and have paid officers. Whatever the level of organization, user groups can be a valuable resource for all levels of experience.

Computer stores usually know about any local groups and can provide information or a copy of the group's newsletter. Attend a meeting and don't be afraid to ask questions. Everyone there remembers their first struggles with the computer and will be happy to spare someone else some of the frustration.

If the group is large enough, it is likely to have *special-interest groups (SIGs)*. These groups often focus on specific software or applications such as networks. Various SIGs can meet after the main meeting to discuss accounting software or the basics of communications.

Your company can encourage users to participate by paying dues and allowing time off to attend meetings. Make sure the company members share their experiences and circulate the user group newsletter.

Hire a Tutor

Casual tutoring occurs all the time in the computing office environment. This learning method has the advantage of being focused on the immediate task and being one-on-one. A disadvantage is that the user may become too dependent on the tutor to solve problems. The help session also uses the tutor's time when this may not be part of the tutor's job.

Consider hiring a professional tutor, probably a computer consultant, to get very customized information. The tutor's responsibility is to help you learn how to solve specific problems and discover new features. A tutor's student should remain at the keyboard as the tutor talks through the solution. The student should take as many notes as necessary to remember the problem and the solution and to share the information with others in the office.

Using Computer-assisted Instruction

Computer-assisted instruction (CAI) software exists for most major applications. Newer programs even include their own tutorials. Microsoft products frequently have very complete tutorials included as part of the software package.

Some of the commercial CAI packages require the learner to use the software program being taught. Other packages run on their own. Quality and flexibility vary from package to package. CAI provides consistent training for users within a work group. A good training combination would be to use CAI to introduce the software and then follow that with specific training sessions.

The problem with CAI (as well as with video training and books, covered in the next sections) is that the user must be motivated to use the tool to get anything from it. Classes and training are scheduled, and the student is bound to learn at least something by sitting in the sessions. With computer-assisted instruction, the learner has to take the time and initiative to sit in front of the computer and learn. The learning process is based on the structure set up by the user.

Here are several suggestions to get the most out of user-structured learning:

✦ Establish a buddy system. Users pair up to discuss their schedules and goals for learning the software.

✦ Create a small reward for completing the course within a certain period of time. While learning something new can be motivating by itself, a nice lunch doesn't hurt.

✦ Set a specific schedule within the work group to use the software. If the CAI program takes approximately six hours to use, assigning each user a specific week helps everyone arrange his or her schedule and stick with it.

✦ For a designated period every week, declare a learning break of one to two hours. Everyone uses CAI, watches a video, studies a computer book, works as a team, or in some way spends time learning something new about computers. Treat this time like a staff meeting, except that everyone remains in his or her office. Allow no calls or interruptions.

✦ Provide some token of completion. While a certificate may cover a hole in the wall, a T-shirt covers more and is useful.

Video Training

Video training is gaining popularity because users can relax in front of the TV while "learning" how to use the computer. For providing an overview of the software or showing examples of what the software can accomplish, video training can be very useful. A tape can provide the more human explanation of what to expect and the general steps of how to get there.

People have come to expect entertainment after popping in a video, but most training tapes come across as pretty dull. There is very little music and few dancing images, and the people on film just talk to the camera. Here are some tips on using video training tapes:

✦ Use the tapes to get a broad picture of what the software does. Don't worry about writing down each step. Just knowing the tasks that can be completed with the software is enough.

✦ Watch the tape in short segments. Unless the material is extremely interesting, most adults have a 15- to 20-minute tolerance level. Some videos are structured to include breaks every 20 or 30 minutes.

✦ Watch the tape in a group. Stop the tape when someone has a general question and see if the other viewers can help answer the question.

✦ Circulate the tape prior to a training session. The tape can provide the basic concepts prior to the class.

✦ Make your own tapes. The hardware to connect a PC to a video cassette deck costs well under $1,000. The video tape will show exactly what appears on the computer screen. (Aiming the camera at the screen works but it creates a very annoying flicker.) The results will be rough but tailored specifically to your work group's needs.

Books

Even with all the high technology available, books are still a convenient way to learn about computers. Sometimes the printed material provided with software is not as clear as it might be. Users with great faith in computer documentation look in the manuals first for answers. More experienced users typically have at least one book in addition to the manuals on each of the major software packages they use regularly.

Here are a few tips on purchasing and using books:

✦ Determine the targeted experience level of the reader. These levels may include beginner, intermediate, advanced, and reference. Unlike shoe sizes, there are no standard measurements for these experience levels, just rough guidelines.

✦ Open the book randomly to a page. Read a few paragraphs on the page and see if they make any sense at all. Take time to repeat this process. If these paragraphs are loaded with words you don't understand, the book may be written for a more experienced audience.

✦ Scan the table of contents. Are the chapter and topic heads descriptive? Can the table of contents help you find what you need?

✦ Look in the index. How large is it? Do the indexed words have multiple cross-references?

✦ Flip through several pages. Does the material have an open look without wasting space? If there is a lot of dense text, is it easy to find the sections you need?

✦ Examine several books on the same topic. Some books are thicker because the publisher uses heavy paper. Look at the final page counts and the density of the text for a better comparison.

✦ Select a question you already know the answer to. See how quickly you can find the answer. Try this several times. If you can verify the answers you already know, you can probably find the answers to questions you don't know.

✦ Don't be afraid to write in your books. Make whatever notes will help you the next time you are confronted by the same problem. Use post-its to mark pages you refer to frequently.

✦ If your books tend to walk away, write your name on the edges. While this may remind you of high school, kids use the same technique for the same reason.

Book prices, like so many other things, continue to increase. But the return on the investment pays off quickly with computer texts. Assume your time is worth $10 an hour. You spend $29.95 on a book about a program you use all the time. If you save three hours in one month by referring to the book, you will have already paid for it; every use after that is free.

Network Maintenance Checklist

Because your network needs and number of users vary, you'll have to decide how frequently you need to perform the following maintenance tasks. In the checklist, indicate which of these tasks should be performed on a daily (D), weekly (W), or monthly (M) basis and who is to perform them.

D	W	M	Who	Maintenance Task
—	—	—	_____	Check the printer paper, ribbon, and toner supplies
—	—	—	_____	Check the image quality on each printer
—	—	—	_____	Check the remaining hard disk space on the server
—	—	—	_____	Perform a total backup of the server
—	—	—	_____	Perform an incremental backup of the server
—	—	—	_____	Defragment the server hard disk
—	—	—	_____	Check user logs for problems
—	—	—	_____	Review total network performance

Summary

Justifiably proud of your success with the network installation, you might think that the hard part is over. It's not. Now you must perform the delicate task of maintaining the network and the users. This chapter covered a few of the maintenance issues on a small network:

✦ Make changes one by one and allow time to return to the previous setup.

✦ Study the load of printers both on and off the network to determine their best use in the office.

✦ Make sure users understand their responsibilities for managing printers.

✦ Maintain an up-to-date map of all the available resources on the network.

✦ Housekeeping is essential for efficient use of the server hard disk.

✦ Backing up the server is easier with a tape drive.

✦ Keep several generations of backups, with at least one copy off-site.

✦ You may need a UPS if your area has problems receiving steady electrical power.

✦ You can increase performance several ways, including fine-tuning the network software and purchasing faster hardware.

✦ Users need to continue learning about their computers and the software they use.

8

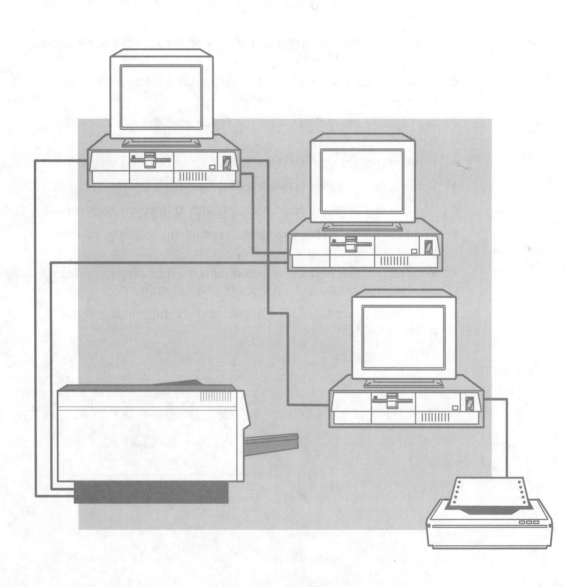

WORKING WITH A CONSULTANT

If you decide not to install the network yourself, you need to hire a network consultant. This chapter provides a step-by-step outline for selecting and dealing with a consultant, including finding the consultant, requesting and negotiating the bid, and managing the project. The extensive worksheet at the end of the chapter helps you deal with all aspects of hiring and working with a consultant to get the best results for your network.

As long as there have been computers, there have been computer consultants. If your computer project is very complicated or requires more time than you have, a consultant may be essential.

Pay for Experience

The consultant has experience to sell—a commodity that can save you time. You, the client, may need to purchase that experience. The money is tangible, easily tracked in the budget process. The consultant's experience is intangible, based mostly on their promises rather than tangible results. While it appears that the client has the upper hand in the transaction, the consultant usually holds the trump card. Money can come from many sources. For the consultant, you are just one source. The experience you need comes from one of just a few sources—a good consultant.

The consultant/client relationship is not necessarily adversarial. But what you think you will get and what you finally have as the result of the consultant's work may be very different. The difference in expectations may result from hiring the consultant in the first place. How can you evaluate someone's expertise when you don't have that expertise yourself? This chapter helps make sure you get what you pay for when you hire a consultant.

In this chapter, a *consultant* is an individual, department, or company you ask to help with your computer project. Even if the helpful party is someone from another department in your company, the principles and ideas mentioned here still apply. In all cases, maintaining good communication is the most important factor for insuring successful results.

Do You Need a Consultant?

You may be interested in installing a network but have decided you don't want to tackle the job alone. Or you may have jumped ahead to this chapter because you want to use a computer consultant for other projects. In any case, you think you will need to get help from someone outside your work group. Here are a few of the reasons why you might want to hire a consultant:

+ No one has the extra time to spend on the project.

+ You want the project completed as quickly as possible.

+ You need to see different ideas for setting up the systems.

+ No one on the staff has any experience with computer hardware.

+ You want "one-stop shopping"—hardware, software, and installation from the same company.

+ You don't have time to train the users.

+ You just don't want to worry about the details.

+ You want assistance while you do the installation.

+ You need backup for problems you can't solve.

+ If you hire an individual, you always know the person you will be dealing with.

+ If you hire a company, they are more likely to provide a wider range of services.

Here are few reasons why you might *not* want to hire a consultant:

+ Hourly fees can range from $25 to $100 or more an hour.

+ If you work with a company, you may see a different face each time someone comes to work on your systems.

+ If you work with an independent consultant, that individual may not always be available when you need him or her.

+ Consultants may know computers and networks, but may not be very good with people.

+ Consultants are likely to be exposed to sensitive data such as payroll and sales information.

+ A consultant may make a mess of things and then just walk away from the project.

This chapter addresses both the positive and negative aspects of using a consultant.

9

Preparing to Hire a Consultant

Before beginning the search for a consultant, you need to decide exactly what you want from him or her. Some factors to consider are the scope of your project, time to completion, the consultant's experience, and additional costs you anticipate for such outside services.

Your project plan should also be as complete as possible. Even if the consultant makes different recommendations, you will at least know enough about the project to make some assessment of those new ideas. For example, if you have already done the preliminary planning steps for your LAN project in this book, you have most of what you need. (Remember that all of this is summarized in the worksheet at the end of this chapter.)

Prepare a summary in a sentence or two to give the consultant a quick idea of the project scope. If you want to consider the project in several steps, list each step. For example, your summary might read, "Install a network with a dedicated server to the five existing systems in the office. Install a common menu system. Provide follow-up support for 30 days."

The amount of time you want the consultant working on your project may range from a few hours a week to full time. This amount, in turn, depends on how much time you can devote to managing the project, how urgent the project is, how much time is required to complete the project, and whether your budget can absorb the extra cost.

You may not know how long the project will take, but you do know how quickly you want the project completed. You'll use this figure when you talk with the consultants. You need to know how much time they have to spend on the project. Consultants are known for their willingness to bite off more than they can chew, figuring life is either feast or famine. They take on too much work and then have to stall clients as they try to finish projects. By establishing the time estimate in the beginning, you can get a simple yes or no answer from the consultants when you ask, "Do you have this much time available within the next week/month/year?"

You also want to list the areas of experience you expect from a consultant. This may be as vague as "has installed networks" to "has written programs using FoxPro LAN 2.0." If you need training and support, include these in this list. You'll use this list as you begin evaluating the consultants you interview. Again, if you don't know specific questions to ask here, let the consultants explain in detail what experience they have.

Some consultants work on an hourly rate. Others bid by the job. Establish what you can really afford and include that in your plan. Comparing the progress of the project with the amount paid can quickly tell you if the original estimate is on track. Once you have talked with several consultants, you'll have a better idea of what to anticipate.

Also list anything else you think might be important to find in a consultant. Will he or she need to do presentations for upper management? If so, you'll want someone with presentation skills. If the consultant will be working with a number of people, can he or she communicate in plain English? If a big rush comes, can the consultant devote extra time to your project?

Your project consultant planning document might look like the one shown in Figure 9-1.

Summary
Install a network with a dedicated server to the five existing systems in the office. Install a common menu system. Provide follow-up support for 30 days.

Time
Devote at least two days for the installation. Weekly three-hour visits for support for the next four weeks. Start the installation by the beginning of next month.

Experience
The consultant will have installed at least two networks using Ethernet cards and coax cable. Be familiar with, and recommend, network software.

Expenses
Estimate 16 hours of installation time and 12 hours of support at $60 an hour, $1,680 total.

Project
consultant
planning
document
Figure 9-1.

Types of Consultants

The term "computer consultant" is very broad since certification is not required; anyone can have business cards printed with a computer consultant title. The actual range of services provided can vary. It is important to know what kind of consultant you are considering because the consultant's services influence his or her recommended "solutions" to your problems.

Resellers and Retailers

Computer resellers/retailers are one of the more prevalent kinds of consultants. They are also called sales representatives or sales consultants. If you talk with someone in a computer store, you know you are talking with a sales rep, however, someone who visits you in your office may not have a name tag to clue you in.

A reseller's job consists of selling you hardware and software. Most of these consultants can evaluate your needs based on a series of questions. They can then sell you all the hardware, software, and services recommended in that evaluation. If you already know what you want, they can provide their best price.

Because resellers make their profit in the mark-up on the items you purchase, you are not likely to get a lot of consulting. Resellers are going to recommend products they carry or can easily purchase and then resell to you. These products may be name brand, or they may be clones containing parts from around the world. In all cases, make sure you obtain the warranty in writing.

If you do use a reseller, get in writing that all the equipment and software will work as promised. For example, if a reseller provides four 386SX systems with 1MB of memory, that consultant should also know that Windows 3.1 will not perform well on these machines. This awareness of compatibility is a good reason to purchase from one source, provided you make that objective known in your discussions with the consultant. You may find this one-stop shopping the easiest way to purchase equipment and software and be reasonably assured that everything works together.

You'll also need to consider the reseller's history. How long have they been in business? How many people work for the company? Do they have a store? Of course, if everyone waited until computer retailers had been in business for a year, the business would never survive. Just keep these factors in mind when making large purchases.

Value Added Reseller

Value added resellers, also known as VARs, sell hardware, software, or a combination of the two. The difference is that the VAR has bundled software or combined packages to perform specific tasks. For example, if you managed several properties, a VAR might sell you a complete computer system containing computers, a LAN, and a property management program. Because VARs are selling this packaged solution, they can guarantee that everything works together.

A VAR is easier to pick from the consulting crowd. Their products are designed for specific markets. They'll make sure you fit within their market before they spend much time talking with you. If you do have a problem they can solve, they'll go to great lengths to convince you they have the solution. If you already have the computer systems, they may be willing to make the LAN connection and install their software.

The VAR solution may be more expensive than other consultants, but it is also likely to be more stable. These consultants plan to keep you as a regular customer because they have provided a specific solution. Their attentiveness is likely to include additional support services, such as staff training and upgrading the software with new releases on an hourly or contract basis.

9

Independent Consultants

You may be looking for someone who sells you only time and experience. In this case, the individual is selling himself or herself and all the experiences he or she has had as a consultant.

You may need this experience for one or more phases in the process of the project. Since different phases require different skills, consider each one as you select your consultant.

Design Consultant

A design consultant may assist you as you decide what you need to accomplish. This consultant helps you determine your goals, evaluate your resources, and chart the path from point A to point B. You may want the consultant to do all the work and then use the consultant's prepared reports as your plan. Alternatively, the consultant may just guide and advise you as you develop your own plan. Experience is a great asset for a design consultant.

Programming Consultant

A programming consultant can write code in one or more computer languages. If you are not sure what language your project will require, the programming consultant is likely to suggest one he or she knows. Programming is not the same as design. Make sure you see working samples of previous projects if the programmer is also going to do the design work.

Support Consultant

The support consultant provides assistance on a wide range of computer-related topics. This individual should be able to install almost any software and provide help with specific programs. Ask to see a list of software the support consultant has experience with before you discuss specific applications. If you need help with XYZ software and the consultant has not worked with XYZ software, you'll have room to negotiate the rates. Also note that some support consultants are better with software, while others handle only hardware problems. A very useful support consultant has a range of software experience and can provide hardware support as well.

Training Consultant

Knowing how to use a program and showing others how to use it are two different skills. A computer consultant may know every trick in the book but not have any idea of how to convey that information. If you need training, make sure you find a consultant with experience in teaching individuals and groups, including material preparation and classroom training.

Locating a Consultant

The best way to locate a consultant is through word-of-mouth. Talk with anyone who has computers and ask if they have ever used a consultant. If they have, ask if they can provide a recommendation and a phone number. Referrals from similar work environments are even more valuable. If you work in the personnel department, try to talk with someone in the personnel department of a similar-sized company. If they worked with someone and didn't care for the results, ask what went wrong. You'll learn from their experience what to watch out for with the consultant you eventually hire.

Computer dealers may be able to provide referrals for consultants. They may work with consultants who arrange purchases on behalf of clients. This referral source may be biased, though. The dealer and consultant may have a strong working relationship. The dealer passes along the consultant's name and the consultant brings the client back to the dealer for any hardware and software purchases. There may be nothing wrong with this arrangement, but it helps to know if it exists before you get too involved with the consultant.

The computer dealer may be able to provide a more specific referral if you already know what hardware and software you are working with. Since dealers advertise the brands they carry, you can select a dealer who carries your current or selected equipment and software. The dealer is more likely to refer someone with experience using those products.

Professional organizations can provide a resource for names. Many computer consultants belong to these groups, several of which are based on the consultants' areas of specialization. Your local library may have a list of local groups and associations. If your business has an organization associated with it, members may be able to refer you to specific consultants or other organizations. While membership in one or more professional organizations suggests that the consultant is active in his or her field, some consultants are not "joiners" and may not belong to any group.

Larger cities have computer user groups. Check the library, phone book, or local computer dealer for the name and phone number. Keep in mind that consultants from user groups may be less experienced that those you locate through professional organizations.

The business section of the phone book provides a wide variety of listings from Computer Equipment to Computer Software Services to Computer System Designers and Consultants. You may want to start with those listings located close to your business. The presence of a large ad may or may not mean that the company is successful. Some consultants have enough business from referrals that they don't even purchase ad space in the phone book. Remember that just because a consultant is not listed in the phone book does not mean he or she is not legitimate.

Selecting the Right Consultant

Don't begin calling consultants until you have gathered at least five names on your list. If you have only one name, it is very easy to take the quick way out and hire the only person you talk with. If you have a list, you will be more inclined to at least contact everyone on that list before making a decision.

Making the Contact

Your first contact with a consultant will be on the phone. You can save everyone's time if you "qualify" the person before asking for an interview. Don't ask, What kind of consulting do you do? Any consultant who figures he or she has a prospective client on the phone will express a wide range of proficiencies. Use your planning list to ask specific questions, such as, Do you install networks? Are you familiar with networks? Do you provide training and support? Also ask general questions, such as, How long have you been in business? and What kind of educational background do you have in computers? If the consultant wants to know what you need, you can be very general at this point. A very "flexible" consultant will just happen to have whatever experience you are looking for.

Since you want your project to get under way sometime soon, availability is important. Don't ask, Are you looking for another client? Most consultants always think they can handle at least one more client. Ask instead, Can you install a network for five users within the next 30 days?

Don't expect to talk about fees or expenses over the phone. There are too many variables for most consultants to offer prices without much information. A few might offer an hourly rate but, as you'll see later in this chapter, this can always be negotiated. If you really want to make sure you have a potential match, describe your project and time frame.

Based on the answers to these questions, decide if you want to invite the consultant for an interview. If you have contacted a large company, specify that you would like to meet with an account representative (salesperson) and a consultant. While the consultant you interview may not actually be the one doing the work, he or she can keep the account rep from promising more than is reasonable.

At this point, you will have talked with at least five consultants by phone. You may want to narrow down the field to three people or companies. Now you need to call each one into your office for an interview.

Interviews

When you interview a consultant, you want to determine if the person can deliver what you really need. You are not hiring this person like you would a new employee. You must be certain that the consultant already knows how to do the work.

Start by explaining that you are talking with a number of consultants. This may prove to be a shock to some. Too many companies consider consultants sequentially: talk to one, hire or not; talk to another one, hire or not. The sense of competition should make them pay more attention to the interviewing process.

The first thing to review is the consultant's experience. If you explain your project first, you may discover that every consultant has exactly the experience you need. If the individual represents a company, ask how many people work in the company. This provides a sense of "depth" in the company. If you are talking with an independent consultant, find out how long that person has been in business. Don't be too concerned if the individual has been a consultant for less than a year, as long as he or she has previous experience with another company.

Ask for at least three references from other clients. If they are not readily available, request that the information be included in the proposal. The consultant should provide names and phone numbers of clients willing to speak for the consultant. You should assume that the consultant has asked permission to use these clients as references. If you discover that the consultant has neglected that little detail, you should question their level of professionalism.

9

Describe your project again and ask, generally, how the consultant would go about solving the problem. If the person declines, saying that is what he or she gets paid for, you'll have to decide for yourself how interested that person is in doing the work. Don't expect any kind of instant quote for the cost of the project. Consultants might provide a price range, based on previous experience, but don't expect to hold them to that estimate.

Ask how soon the consultant or company could begin working on the project. Make it clear that you are not asking them to actually begin the work and that you still must make a final decision. But part of making that decision is knowing if they can begin within the next week or if you'll have to wait a month while they finish other projects. This may be vague because the consultant's schedule may be based on a lot of variables. If the consultant expresses an interest in starting tomorrow, you know he or she is not very busy or has decided that your project is more appealing than his or her current work.

If at this point you decide that this consultant could handle the project, offer him or her a chance to prepare a quote for the job. The consultant should then begin asking you questions to determine the specifics of the project. The more detailed the questions are, the better. The consultant is trying to make sure he or she will present a solution tailored to your problem. If the questions are vague, you are likely to get a standard "cookie-cutter" solution.

At the conclusion of the interview, ask how long it will take for the consultant to return a proposal. A week is reasonable, depending on the size of the project. If the project is very complicated, the person may ask for another interview to gather more information. Again, this suggests that the consultant really wants to understand what you need.

Remind the prospective consultant that the estimated cost of the project is another factor in the decision-making process. Point out that you are also considering the individual's experience and timetable in your selection. Give him or her a specific date by which you will make the final decision. If you offer to notify the consultant even if you don't choose him or her, you may find it easier to call the "runner-up" if your first choice falls through.

Following Up References

When you talk with the consultant's references, you can assume that he or she would not provide the names of dissatisfied clients. The best kind of questions are descriptive and objective. Here are a few:

+ How long has the consultant worked for you?

+ How did you locate the consultant? (The person may be related or a friend.)

+ What was the project or in what specific ways did the consultant help? (Is this the same business you are in?)

+ What is the consultant's working style? Was he or she on time for appointments? Did he or she leave the work areas neat? Did he or she meet deadlines?

+ How well did the consultant keep you informed about the project's progress?

Subjective answers provide information if you make the questions specific. Just asking, Were you satisfied with the consultant's work? is too broad. Ask questions like these instead:

+ Did the consultant respond to your questions and concerns?

+ How well do you think the consultant works with people?

+ Would you use this consultant for training?

+ What do you think is this consultant's greatest strength?

+ What is the consultant's most noticeable weakness?

+ Do you anticipate using this consultant again?

These are a lot of questions, and answering them may take more time than someone is willing to spend. Have your questions written down before phoning. Put the important questions first so you can get the most critical information if the referral cuts the call short.

9

Proposal Basics

Now you have from three to five proposals on your desk. Proposals vary in quality and content. Some consist of a one- or two-page spreadsheet showing the items, quantities, and total costs. Installation and support times may or may not be broken out of the total. If the consultant is selling you the equipment, he or she may have included the cost of installation in the margin. You may choose to accept this bottom-line type of proposal if you trust the consultant completely.

If you want more details or expect to negotiate with the consultant, the proposal should contain at least the following information. (You may want to provide this list of points for the consultant to address.)

- A brief description of your company or department
- A statement of the problem
- The proposed solution
- The existing equipment and software
- Recommended additional equipment and software
- Price quotes if the consultant is providing the equipment, or price estimates and a recommended vendor
- Specific services the consultant will provide, including installation and support
- The costs of that installation and support
- Specific parts of the project the client is responsible for
- A time frame for the provision of these services
- A payment schedule
- The length of time the proposal is offered
- The name and phone number of the individual who prepared the proposal
- A summary of the consultant's work experience
- A list of at least three references, including phone numbers

The purpose of the proposal is to let you, the client, know that the consultant understands what the project entails. It need not be lengthy. Be careful to judge the content of the proposal. The consultant is not likely to be an English major. On the other hand, obvious misspellings or sloppy presentation of the material suggests poor attention to detail.

Some consultants are not willing to provide a proposal if they feel you are just using them to get ideas about what you want to do. Present a solid outline of your needs. The consultant should be able to get a good picture after asking a few questions. If you are vague or really have no idea what you want to do, the consultant may suggest that a complete study and planning document be prepared before a proposal can be offered. The consultant can reasonably charge for this service since the interview and report preparation could take from 5 to 20 hours.

A Sample Proposal

Figure 9-2 shows a sample proposal based on the client's expressed need for help installing the network. The network plan and the hardware and software have already been selected.

Negotiating the Proposal

Do not assume that a proposal is a final offer. Very few consultants will mention that their proposal is flexible. In fact, you may have room to negotiate every item in the proposal. Consider that piece of paper a working document and make a counter-proposal.

If you have more than one consultant providing a proposal, you'll have a way to compare the costs and time estimates. If you have narrowed down the field to one consultant, you may not want to push too hard. The consultant can decline to participate any further, and you'd have to start over.

Negotiating is an art and a science. You can easily spend more time than it is worth to rework a proposal. On the other hand, you may be able to spend just a few minutes and save hundreds of dollars. Here are a few suggestions for working with a consultant's proposal:

9

Proposal for: XYZ Widget Company
From: ABC Consulting
Date: July 9, 1993

Summary

ABC Consulting recommends the purchase of a five-station peer-to-peer network, appropriate cards, and cable. An additional 386 system should be added to the four currently in use. The new server should also include a tape drive backup system. We will install all cables, cards, and software within a week after the outside vendor delivery. An additional 30 days of support will be provided. Total cost for installation and support is $X,XXX.

Introduction

The XYZ Widget Company's personnel department has been keeping employee records on one computer system for the past two years. The software maintains all the data on each employee, including payroll and health records. When anyone needs access to those records, he or she uses the one computer system containing the data. Of the remaining three systems, two are used by clerical staff and the third is located in the department manager's office. The secretaries each have a laser printer attached. The other two systems have dot matrix printers attached.

According to Jim Mains, the department computer coordinator, he backs up the system with the critical data at least once a week. No one backs up data on the other hard disks unless Jim comes in on a Saturday.

Current Problem

The company has expanded and everyone in the personnel department now needs access to the records at the same time. The software has a network upgrade. Depending on the report, users need to access either a laser or a dot matrix printer. Backups of all systems need to be performed on a regular basis.

Proposed Solution

All of the current systems are 286-based with the exception of one XT. While they are adequate for the workload, a more powerful computer should be installed as the server/workstation. With a peer-to-peer system, all five systems could use any of the printers attached to the computers with little effort. The system currently containing the employee database should be relocated into the office of the individual who has the greatest need for database access.

Once the network is installed, all users will have access to the data on the server. All users will be able to print to one of the four available printers. All systems can be backed up to the tape drive in the server. The server will also function as a workstation.

A sample proposal
Figure 9-2.

Current Equipment

This list represents the equipment currently in the department and the location of that equipment:

- ✦ AT system with laser printer (Joan's office)
- ✦ AT system with laser printer (Jake's office)
- ✦ AT system with dot matrix printer (copy room)
- ✦ XT system with dot matrix printer (Jim's office)

Additional Equipment

The following list represents the recommended equipment as well as estimated costs. You may purchase this equipment to specifications, or ABC Consulting will help you locate a reputable dealer with good prices.

386, monochrome VGA, 200MB HD, 4MB memory	X,XXX
500MB tape drive backup	XXX
5 network cards	X,XXX
Cable and connectors	XXX
Network software	X,XXX
Estimated total	$XX,XXX

As part of the installation, we will help you upgrade your employee database program to the network version. You will be responsible for purchasing that program prior to our installation visit.

Services Provided

As mentioned, we will help you locate a vendor for the equipment if you like. Our primary responsibilities include the following:

1. Unpack, set up, and test the 386 system.
2. Install cards in the 386 and one 286, run temporary cable, install and test the server and workstation versions of the software.
3. Toss cable to each station location.
4. Move the 286 system to an office.
5. Install remaining network cards and attach to the server.
6. Test all cable connections.
7. Install user accounts and set up printer server locations.
8. Install employee database system and test it.
9. Provide a one-hour network orientation session for all users.
10. Provide 30 days of telephone and on-site support for the network software.

Total cost for this service will be $X,XXX.
Additional support will be available for $XX per hour after the 30 days have elapsed.

9

Client Responsibilities

The client will be responsible for the cable planning, user access levels, menu modifications, and use of the employee database program after initial installation. The client is expected to test the network and report problems to the consultant within the 30-day contract period. Any problems reported after the 30-day period will be resolved at the standard hourly rate.

Time Frame and Payment

We can install the network within one week after all the equipment has been delivered. Initial installation will take a full day. We recommend that the network training session be conducted within two days of the installation. This proposal is valid for 60 days from this date.

One-half of the total payment for services is expected within 10 days after the LAN has been installed. Final payment is due 30 days after the network has been installed. We will not purchase equipment or supplies as part of the service agreement.

Submitted by

Jesse Johnson

Jesse Johnson
ABC Consulting
5678 Harmony Way
Evansville, IN 47715
812-555-4125

(Business brochure and references attached)

A sample
proposal
(*continued*)
Figure 9-2.

Don't Nickel and Dime   Be careful that you are suggesting adjustments to areas you are really interested in changing. For example, changing the completion date from 30 to 25 days is not likely to be worth the effort. Changing completion from 60 to 30 days may be.

Don't Reopen Settled Issues   The first pass defines the issues you want to change. Don't add new items on the next pass.

Don't Push Beyond Recovery   Everyone has limits. Remember that you may have to compromise also. If you push too hard on too many issues, the consultant may just decide not to work with you.

Do Ask Questions   Ask for clarification on anything you don't understand in the proposal. This can occur before or during the negotiations. Once a point is questioned, the clarification can then be negotiated.

Do Respond Quickly   If at all possible, and with a modest-sized proposal, response times could be as little as one day on both ends. If both sides work this way, the final project specifications should be done within a week. Fax machines are very handy as part of this process.

Do Agree on a Timetable   State the length of time you think the negotiations should take. The consultant may be just as anxious to start on the project as you are.

Do Request a Final Copy   Make sure the consultant prepares a final copy of the proposal incorporating all verbal agreements and items discussed since the original proposal.

Keep in mind that the more expensive the proposal, the more time you should spend working on it. A proposal to provide one computer and software installation might be only $2,500. There is little room to negotiate that quote, although you can try. A proposed network installation including a server, six cards, cabling, and installation might easily be over $10,000. There may be more leeway there.

9

Making the Commitment

Once you have accepted a final offer verbally, send a letter stating the same thing. State the payment schedule and reiterate that final payment is based on satisfactory completion of the work. If the project is to take more than a week or two, indicate the specific reporting requirements, explained in detail in the section "Managing the Project" later in this chapter.

Include in the letter the project timetable, making note of anything happening at the company that might affect the days or times the consultant can work. List people the consultant may need to work with and include their phone numbers.

Less Formal Proposals

By now, you may imagine that hiring a consultant is a complicated process. It need not be, depending on the level of trust you have in the individual or company you hire. If you really believe that the first consultant you interview will do what he or she promises, for the price quoted, you need not go through any of these steps. But all too often, clients discover that what they thought they were getting did not come close to what the consultant provided.

Even if you don't go through as much paperwork, at least get an outline of the tasks the consultant expects to do. Then prepare a letter explaining the payment schedule, reserving the right to withhold payment until the work has been completed to your satisfaction.

Managing the Project

Hiring a consultant does not mean that you give up control of the project. Stay informed during each phase of the project. This may mean a weekly half-hour meeting during which the consultant explains what has transpired since the last meeting. A more exacting method is to require a written report every week or before the next payment is issued. Even if you do not understand all the details provided, you have a better chance of measuring progress on the project.

Staying in touch also lets the consultant know that *you* must approve any major changes. If the consultant makes a decision without talking with you and that decision costs more money or time, you can appropriately decline to pay for that deviation in the project plan. While you probably can't make the consultant foot the entire extra cost, if the change increases the amount of time the consultant spends on the project, you shouldn't have to pay the full amount.

On the other hand, if you constantly expand the scope of the project or make changes to approved work, the consultant can reasonably charge for the extra time required. If you do make changes, ask if that will add to the time and expense. Also ask for new projections for completion. Your changes will cost money and extend the completion date.

When decisions change the path of the project, make sure someone explains the reasons for the change and the results. This information may be recorded in your weekly progress meetings or contained in the progress reports the consultant submits. If the change will cost extra, make sure everyone understands how much you approve for the additional expense. Making a note of approval on the written report and making a copy for the consultant is a good approach.

Set Timetables

The original proposal should contain a timetable for completion of the project. If it doesn't, make sure you include one in your letter of acceptance. Without this agreement, consultants can work on the project anytime they want. They can use your project as a filler for when they don't have any other work.

If either you or the consultant needs to change the schedule, make sure everyone agrees. Again, the weekly update is the place to note and approve those changes.

A payment schedule should be determined at the same time the project timetable is established. Some consultants expect full payment as soon as the hardware has been installed. Unless you are sure everything is working well, you need not agree to pay the full amount at that point. You may want to pay one-half after the first installation and the rest in 30 days, when you are sure the system works as promised. All of this should be negotiated before the project begins.

If an independent consultant is doing a great deal of work for you, 15 or more hours a week, payment of the invoice may be his or her only income. You can express appreciation for the work your consultant is doing by making sure the invoice is processed as quickly as possible. Tossing the invoice into the system when you know payments take 30 days or more will not endear you to your consultant. Quick processing will earn you extra points from the consultant's view. Those points come in very handy if you get stuck later and need quick help from him or her.

Providing Assistance

You may choose to stay even more involved with the project than by receiving weekly updates. Depending on the project and the consultant, you may want to help where and when permitted. In essence, you work for and under the guidance of the consultant.

Chapter 3 lists some things you might be able to do to assist the consultant. Make sure these tasks are understood in the initial agreement.

Some consultants will take the extra time to explain what they are doing. But they may require more time for the project or charge a slightly higher fee than you might expect. Again, let the consultant know if you want this to be part of the agreement. If you are interested, this exchange of information can be very valuable to you later.

Cutting Your Losses

If you suspect that the project has gotten off track, discuss this with your consultant *immediately.* Don't wait around to check out your hunch. The sooner you confront the issue, the less damage done. If you keep track of the project on a regular basis, this discussion should be minimal and little effort will be required to reset the course.

If you have let the problem build, you may need more drastic action. Be prepared to drop the project. Rest assured, the consultant will be so inclined if the conversation gets too sticky. If there is money outstanding, pay only for the amount of work you actually feel the consultant has completed. If you have paid ahead of the work actually done, you may ask for it back but don't expect the consultant to "work off" the difference.

If the conversation is extremely contentious, don't allow the consultant to return to the equipment. It is sad but true that an experienced computer user can destroy all the files on a system within minutes. Since your consultant is likely to have complete access to the files, that damage could be extensive.

Recovery from a consulting project gone awry takes time and additional experience. Try to learn from the situation and note what you could have done to prevent it. List the problems you observed with the consultant. This inventory will help you when you elect to hire another consultant to restart the project.

You can also prepare for this event, as noted later in this chapter in the section "Backup Consulting." But make sure you've done your prep work before you've told your current consultant to "take a hike."

Continuing Support

Once the project has been completed, problems are still likely to occur. After you have attempted to solve the problem, you may need to return to the original consultant or another consultant for assistance. Regular and reliable support is an essential part of almost any ongoing computer project.

Determine the Level of Support

The level of support is frequently misunderstood. For example, the sample proposal from the middle of this chapter stipulates "30 days of telephone and on-site support." What does this phrase really mean?

✦ Can you call the consultant and have someone come over right away? Or does the consultant try to solve the problem on the phone and then send someone out if that doesn't work?

✦ If you're using an independent consultant, how can you reach him or her in an emergency? Does he or she have anyone for backup? What do you do if this person goes on vacation?

✦ How quickly does your call get routed to someone who can answer your questions?

✦ How long do you wait for an on-site visit?

All these terms may be spelled out in the proposal. If the proposal indicates a specific amount of time, the support should be part of the total cost. If it is additional, you must know the hourly rate. If the support is not specified, you should get the terms in writing before agreeing to the proposal or hourly rate. In many cases, both parties can determine the urgency of the request. The response time can satisfy the client and can be met without excessive hardship on the consultant.

Continued Support

Almost anyone who uses computers gets stuck with a problem he or she can't solve. By establishing an ongoing relationship with a consultant, you have a ready source for help with even little problems. Since the consultant already knows who you are and you know the consultant's areas of expertise, the phone call to resolve the problem may be very short.

In many cases, you locate and use a consultant for large projects. The consultant then continues to help with additional problems even if he or she is not related to the original project. You will have an agreement with the consultant concerning the hourly rate for phone time and the minimum rate for an on-site visit. Even if you don't have a large project, you might consider locating and interviewing a consultant to use on a regular basis.

However you begin using a consultant, you may want to encourage him or her to make suggestions about your use of both hardware and software. A good consultant is always reading about the latest products and talking with other clients about their experiences with new equipment. This "cross-pollination" between users helps all the consultant's clients.

But keep in mind that the consultant may be interested in "upgrading" your systems because that means more work for him or her. Be very careful if the consultant wants to sell you the item. As long as these products really do solve problems or increase productivity, they are worth considering. You may not have known about the products without your consultant's knowledge of the computer industry and your computing environment.

Backup Consulting

A problem frequently cited by system managers is the loss of a consultant or company. This may occur abruptly if the consultant goes out of business, leaves the area, or changes careers. Or this loss may occur gradually if the consultant takes on larger projects and does not have time for old clients. Whatever the reason, you lose the experience the consultant had with your systems.

A very reasonable request is for the consultant to make a list of alternate consultants. Most consultants know several other colleagues, at least by reputation. Since your consultant has your best interests at heart, the list should contain some helpful people or companies. You can explain that this request does not imply that you are dissatisfied with the current work, just that you want to plan for any unexpected events. With such a list, you would at least know whom to call if your consultant was hit by a truck.

Along with this list, you may ask the consultant to prepare a report detailing your systems, using whatever technical terms make the report most helpful to another consultant. The two or three hours you pay for now could save you several days of struggle if you suddenly have to hire a new consultant.

Paying for Services

The consultant provides goods and services. You provide payment. If the consultant renders these services in a timely manner and to your satisfaction, you should provide payment for those services, also in a timely manner. But don't feel that you have to pay the consultant immediately if the invoice contains just a date and an amount. You need to know what you have received.

Consultant Invoices

The physical items a consultant supplies are easily noted. If the consultant lists three computers, you can count three new computers. Any invoice for equipment and software should list each item you have purchased. An exemplary invoice contains the serial numbers for each item as well.

The consultant may have purchased the items from different vendors. For example, the monitor may come from NEC and the system unit may be a clone. Each item with a unique warranty should be included on the invoice. That piece of paper is the only way you can prove the purchase date if you do need warranty service. If the consultant states that he or she provides the warranty service, get the length and details of that warranty in writing before paying the invoice.

Invoices for services are much harder to validate. Basically, you trust the consultant concerning the times listed. If you have been talking with your consultant on a regular basis, you should have a good idea of how much work has been completed with each invoice. If you have not been managing the project, you will pay that invoice on pure faith that the project is making progress. At the least, the invoice should show specific blocks of time and a brief summary of the tasks performed.

If you are not satisfied with the work, you have every right to delay payment of the invoice. In this case, you need to explain, in writing, exactly what you require before making the payment. The requirement may be a request for a more detailed invoice or further assurances that the work has actually been done.

If the consultant is billing you in increments, make sure you are satisfied with each invoice. Consultants have been known to present invoices ahead of the actual progress and then leave when the client expresses dissatisfaction with the actual results.

A Sample Invoice

The invoice shown in Figure 9-3 represents a block of time from a consultant writing a database program. The consultant also provided the software.

Prompt Payments Help

The smaller the consultant's company, the more important timely payment will be. If the consultant is self-employed, your checks may represent his or her sole income during a long stretch of work done for you. If your company is small enough, you may be able to honor the invoice as soon as it is presented, assuming you are satisfied with the work. As mentioned, small consultants remember this courtesy and are likely to respond very quickly the next time you need help.

Worksheet

The following worksheet will help you make decisions related to using a consultant. If you have completed a number of the previous

Invoice for: XYZ Widget Company
From: ABC Consulting
Date: August 26, 1993

I have installed the LAN version of FoxPro 2.0 on the network. Attached are the mock-up reports based on your original designs. I'll begin
defining the record structures and entry screens after you have approved these samples.

Date	Time	Total	Activity
8/12	9:30 - 12:30	3.00	Installed FoxPro and tested at all stations
8/13	10:00 - 3:00	5.00	Prepared 8 sample reports
8/14	9:00 - 12:00	3.00	Prepared basic menu structures

Consulting time	11.00 hours @ XX.XX	XXX.XX
Copy of FoxPro LAN 2.0 SN:3420323		X,XXX.XX
Total due		X,XXX.XX

Based on our original estimate of the time required to complete the
project, the 11 hours represents 7% of the total 150 hours. As always,
prompt payment of this invoice is appreciated.

Sincerely,

Jesse Johnson

Jesse Johnson

A sample
invoice
Figure 9-3.

9

worksheets, you'll have some of the work already done. Each part of the
worksheet represents the steps covered in this chapter.

Do You Need a Consultant?

Use the following checklist to determine if you need a consultant. The
more check marks on the list, the more likely you are to benefit from a
consultant's services.

___ No one has extra time for the project.

___ The project must be completed quickly.

___ You don't know how to proceed.

___ No one has the required computer experience.

___ You want "one-stop shopping."

___ You don't have time to train the users.

___ You don't want to worry about the details.

___ You want help while you plan and install the system.

___ You need a resource for problems you can't solve.

Those "Yes" answers may be countered by this "No" check list:

___ Your budget is extremely tight.

___ You have very sensitive data in the computer.

___ You don't have time to manage a consultant.

___ You just *know* a consultant will mess things up.

What Is the Project?

Prepare a two- or three-sentence summary of the project. Decide when you would like the project completed. List specific programs you already use or plan to use. Estimate how much you can afford to spend on the project.

What Type of Consultant Do You Need?

Use the following questions to help in your search for a consultant:

✦ Do you already know what you want to purchase? (Reseller)

✦ Do you have a problem unique to your type of business? (VAR)

✦ Do you need help with design, programming, or training? (Consultant)

Do You Have Your Names?

Try to get at least five names before you begin calling. Prepare a list of consultants and include the following:

Name
Company
Phone
Fax
Referral source
First impression

What Do You Ask the Consultant?

Prepare a list of questions to ask over the phone. These questions might include

✦ How long have you been in business?

✦ How many people are in your company?

✦ Will I deal with the same person all the time?

✦ Where did that person get his or her experience?

✦ What do you specialize in?

✦ In general, what are your hourly rates?

✦ Do you have referrals, other clients I can talk with?

✦ Are you primarily a reseller, consultant, or both?

✦ What software packages do you specialize in?

✦ Can you do programming? What languages?

✦ Can you provide training? Give some examples.

9

Questions for the interview at your office might include

✦ (After describing the project) Is this something that interests you?

✦ What other projects like this have you worked on?

✦ How soon would you be able to work on this project?

✦ How much time could you then devote to the project?

✦ In general, how would you handle this project?

✦ How soon could you prepare a proposal?

✦ Do you have experience with management presentations?

Which Proposal Meets Your Needs?

Once you have several proposals to compare, you'll have a better idea of the quality. Use the following questions as a guideline:

✦ Does the proposal summarize your company and the project?

✦ Does the proposal outline the solution?

✦ Will you be able to see those results?

✦ Are the recommendations clear?

✦ Do you know who is providing the additional equipment?

✦ Are the prices quoted estimates or the final price?

✦ Does the proposal include a list of the services to be provided?

✦ When will these services be provided?

✦ When is payment expected?

✦ What are you, the client, responsible for?

✦ How long is the proposal offered?

✦ Is a summary of the company included?

✦ Do you know exactly whom to contact for further questions?

Is There Room to Negotiate?

Review the proposals for areas you need to negotiate. Make a copy of the proposal and mark the areas you want changed. Rank each point in order of importance. If the time frame is critical, that is ranked first. If the total cost is more critical, that becomes the most important. When you begin the negotiation, over the phone or in person, work on the lower ranked points first. You can easily give in on those points. By the time the you reach the more important points, you'll have "given in" on several points and the consultant will find it easier to let you "win" on some of the important issues.

How Will You Manage the Project?

Before you notify the consultant, you need to decide how you want to manage the project. You'll outline those requirements in your letter of acceptance. You might require a weekly meeting. You might prefer just a summary with each invoice. Whatever the case, state this in writing. If the project is a one-shot installation, repeat what you expect to be able to do at the conclusion of the project.

Also remember to specify that payment is based on acceptable performance on the project. It is easier to start tough and get easy than it is to start easy and then have to get tough.

Can You Terminate the Arrangement?

Can you make the decision to fire the consultant? (Find someone to help if necessary.) Do you have an emergency plan in case something happens? (Remember your original list of consultants.)

Will You Need Additional Support?

Part of your planning should include a list of potential problems. If you don't have any idea what kinds of problems you'll have, ask your consultant. Consultants make their living solving problems and can easily provide a list of ongoing issues. You'll have to decide if you want to keep the consultant involved in the project. Remember that if you do stay in touch, the consultant is likely to make suggestions for improvements to your system.

What Problems Might Occur with Payment?

To reduce the chances of delay and to maintain goodwill, try to know the following before that first or subsequent invoice lands on your desk:

✦ Have the project expenses already been approved?

✦ Will there be any unusual processing required for the invoice?

✦ What is required on the invoice for it to be considered valid? Date? Amount? Company? EIN or SSN? Individual authorization? Hours and dates of service?

✦ Does the vendor need to complete a specific form for payment?

✦ Is the bookkeeping department going on vacation for two weeks?

✦ Can you hand-carry the invoice for approvals to speed up processing?

✦ Do you know how to track the invoice in the event of a question?

Summary

When you hire a consultant, you are purchasing time and experience. You need to get the most value for your dollar. To do this you need to:

✦ Decide if you really need a consultant.

✦ Know what you expect a consultant to do.

✦ Find the right consultant for the job.

✦ Select from several possible consultants or companies.

✦ Negotiate important points in the proposals.

✦ Notify the consultant and provide written expectations for reporting and invoice payment.

✦ Keep track of the project.

✦ Be prepared to terminate the project if necessary.

✦ Anticipate additional services you might need from the consultant.

✦ Pay the consultant in a timely manner.

INDEX/GLOSSARY

server files, 192
user, 36
Base memory address, 137
Batch file, startup, 156
BBS (bulletin board)
help, 57
virus spread, 190
BNC connectors, 75
crimps, 126
illustration, 138
making, 137
Boards. *See* Cards.
Bomb, virus Program designed to cause damage to the system on a specified date. 189
Books, purchasing, 209
Boot, 97
remote PROM, 137
Boot failure, 131
Borland, 165, 170
Breathing filter, 127
Bridge Device to connect two or more servers.
illustration, 6
Bucket, 8
Building code, 85, 105, 142, 145
Bus structure, 69
Bus topology Stations are connected in a long string with one or more servers anywhere along that string. 78, 84

C

C000h, 137
Cable
backbone, 75
coaxial, 74
conduits, 142
connection failure, 32, 86

estimating, 71, 85
fiber optic, 77
flat ribbon, 79
help, 54, 141
installing, 141
length limits, 105
making connectors, 137
9-wire, 79
other routes, 146
plenum, 75
PVC, 75
ribbon, 79-80
running down wall, 144
shielded, 80
stripping pliers, 139
through walls, 145
tie-downs, 145
tools, purchase, 75
topology, 104
twisted-pair, 72, 76, 144
CAI (computer assisted instruction) Lessons given on the computer. May include additional materials such as video tapes and manuals. 207
Call ID, 24
CAPTURE command, 58
Cards
conflicts, 132
drivers, 156
dual port, 82
8-bit, 130
I/O, 82
inserting damaged, 131
installing, 128
music, 132
network, 69
nonessential, 134
not found, 160
problems, 132

D

T